Patsy and Mike

Tom and Nancy   Patsy and Mike

The LORD is my shepherd.
I shall not want.
² He makes me lie down in green pastures.
He leads me beside quiet waters.
³ He restores my soul;
He guides me in the paths of righteousness
For His name's sake.

⁴ Even though I walk through the valley of the shadow of death,
I fear no evil, for You are with me.
Your rod and Your staff, they comfort me.
⁵ You prepare a table before me in the presence of my enemies.
You have anointed my head with oil. My cup overflows.
⁶ Surely goodness and lovingkindness will follow me all the days of
my life,
And I will dwell in the house of the LORD forever.

~ Psalm 23

Dying Happy

A conversation between two men, each facing his terminal cancer with true Christian happiness!

Mike McKinnon
and
Tom Northcott

Dying Happy!

Increasing Our Joy and Peace
As We Leave This World

Mike McKinnon
Tom Northcott

Dying Happy
by Mike McKinnon and Tom Northcott

Printed in the United States of America

ISBN 9781498402385

Cover Design: Mike McKinnon
Text Design: Cheryl Fitch

For more copies of this book, contact

Pleroma Bible Church
PO Box 1178
Tullahoma, TN 37388
www.PleromaBibleChurch.org

www.xulonpress.com

For God so loved the world that He gave His only begotten Son,

that whoever believes in Him shall not perish but have eternal life.

For God did not send the Son into the world to judge the world

but that the world might be saved through Him.

~ John 3:16-17

If we confess our sins,

He is faithful and righteous to forgive us our sins

and to cleanse us from all unrighteousness.

~ I John 1:9

Therefore, being always of good courage, and knowing that while we are at home in the body we are absent from the Lord—for we walk by faith, not by sight—we are of good courage, I say, and prefer rather to be absent from the body and to be at home with the Lord. Therefore we also have as our ambition, whether at home or absent, to be pleasing to Him. For we must all appear before the judgment seat of Christ, so that each one may be recompensed for his deeds in the body, according to what he has done, whether good or bad.

~ 2Corinthians 5:6-10

TABLE OF CONTENTS

TABLE OF CONTENTS

Dying Happy!

Increasing Our Joy and Peace As We Leave This World

You may well be asking yourself why two sixtyish males, one from Albany, Georgia, by way of Enterprise, Alabama, one from Tullahoma, Tennessee, by way of Indianapolis, Indiana, one a sign and print shop owner, one an oral and maxillofacial surgeon, both retired, chose to write a book.

Both of us are in the latter stages of incurable cancer. But we have no fear of dying. In fact, we are filled with more joy, peace, contentment, and thanksgiving than we have ever known. We want you to have that same incomparable level of happiness as you go through life's inevitable suffering.

And you can.

We'll show you how easy it is to super-size your joy and peace.

Our story, the one that led to this book, began last July 4 at a Bible conference in Tullahoma. While we had known each other casually for several years, we'd never sat down to talk until we found ourselves enjoying lunch together on a screened in porch, looking down on the Tennessee countryside. Our pleasure turned to downright joy when we realized that though we were both dying, we both enjoyed incredible happiness and peace, much more so than at any other time in our lives. Our camaraderie increased when Tom and his wife Nancy brought granddaughters Reagan and Renee to the Albany Bible Church Labor Day conference. Two months later, when Mike and his wife Patsy decided to include Pleroma Bible Church in their "farewell tour", which culminated in a visit to an aunt and uncle in New York and included various friends and family on the way, they stayed with Tom and Nancy. On the last day of that visit, Mike turned to Tom and said, "You've finished bush hogging the land for the new church building; you've spread the mulch piles around your house, so what do you plan to do with the rest of your life?" Tom's response was a puzzled look. Grinning, Mike asked, "What would you think about writing a book?" The puzzlement increased. "A book that will help others who are suffering have the same joy and peace we have." Enlightenment dawned. The more we talked, the more excited we became. Time was short for both of us so two weeks later Mike and Patsy were back in Tullahoma, recorder in hand, and this book had its beginning.

We chose a conversational style for our book because the Bible is filled with encouraging conversations that glorified God. After Paul's years in Arabia being taught by Jesus Christ Himself—in conversations, we assume—Paul visited Peter for fifteen days. Imagine the enlightenment, encouragement, and comfort they both received during those discussions! Jonathan and David encouraged each other before David was forced to flee for his life from Jonathan's father, King Saul. Mary and Elizabeth encouraged each other as they awaited the arrival of God's special gifts to them and to the world, our Savior Jesus Christ and His prophesied herald John the Baptizer. As with Joseph, Moses, Hannah, Daniel, Mary, and so many other Bible greats, utmost encouragement comes from our conversations with God our Father in prayer. Thus, the conversational format of this book was born.

We will begin our book with the prayer Tom prayed for us as we embarked on this exciting project.

Dear heavenly Father, Thank you for this glorious day. Thank you for bringing us one day closer to eternity with you. Thank you for the many privileges and blessings we have received throughout our lives in preparation for the end of this part of our lives, leading to eternity with you. We pray that through your grace and the filling of the Holy Spirit, we will have the wisdom to express our thoughts as You would have us, that we will be of use for your service and glory through our lives and eventually through the lives of others. In Jesus name, Amen

Now, let's find out how you can have the greatest happiness you have ever known!

Chapter 1

You Mean This Thing Is Incurable?

*THEREFORE WE DO NOT LOSE HEART, BUT THOUGH <u>our outer man is decaying</u>,
yet our inner man is being renewed day by day. For momentary, light affliction is producing for us an eternal weight of glory far beyond all comparison,
while we look not at the things which are seen but at the things which are
not seen for the things which are seen are temporal, but the things which are
not seen are eternal. 2Corinthians 4:16-18[1]*

Tom: My cancer came first so I'll start. On my fifty-first birthday,
when I had my annual physical examination, my internist found the
initial signs of prostate cancer. I was busy so I put off having blood
drawn for several months. After all, I could have been a poster boy
for anti-cancer living: daily exercise (both aerobic and weight training), good nutrition, and no processed or fast foods. I'd never inhaled
even one breath of cigarette smoke. According to the powers that be
in the world, I shouldn't get sick, much less get cancer! Finally, though,
I found an hour and found also that my PSA, the test that measures
prostate cancer, was 170 something, not the normal 0-4.

Mike: So following man's ideas for healthy living hadn't worked for
you.

---

1   All Bible references are from the New American Standard Bible (NASB).

1

Tom: Definitely not. I was sick, very sick even though I felt fine. The urologist I went to next was an old friend. He'd played keyboard and I'd played the drums in a band composed mainly of medical professionals. We'd spent many fun hours together. He put me through another round of tests, including more scans. I was busy with my day to day office routine, so Nancy took his phone call giving the results. She was the first to learn that my diagnosis was incurable, inoperable, metastatic to the regional lymph nodes, advanced stage prostate cancer with a life expectancy of 3 to 5 years. We found out later the doctors didn't expect me to live much past the new year. Nancy broke the news to me about the severity of the cancer. She was able to handle it calmly, and her faith rubbed off on me. The urologist suggested we take a previously planned cruise, our first, and think through the therapy options he'd given us.

Mike: Sounds like your doctor was as relaxed as you.

Tom: He was. His reason for not worrying was the same as ours. He trusts the Lord. He's a good man, easy to talk with, as well as a skilled physician. He didn't think I'd live long and wanted us to enjoy one last time together before our lives were forever changed. He was right about the cruise. Nancy and I had a great time. We relaxed, enjoyed being together, discussed our alternatives, and decided to take the surgery option that would eliminate all testosterone from my body. I didn't have any symptoms when I was diagnosed, but that surgery began sapping my energy and gradually changed my lifestyle. Six months after the surgery, the cancer was still present but in complete remission. My PSA was less than zero. Don't ask me how that was possible!

Mike: You mean there was no outward appearance of the cancer? It was dormant.

Tom: Right. The doctors were amazed. In fact, my urologist told us later that he gets out my initial scans at least once a year to convince himself that his diagnosis was correct, that the cancer really was as nasty as he remembered. That aggressive cancer remained in remission for twelve years! Remember the three to five year prediction and the one year expectation? The Lord was clearly in control. After the miracle was obvious to everyone, the cancer became active again, spreading to my bones. During the past five years, I have been treated with an experimental oral medication and two types of chemotherapy. We monitor the cancer's progress monthly and treat the side-effects and symptoms. Seventeen years later and I'm still here. Makes me glad I didn't worry even at the beginning.

Mike: Useless stuff, worry. Such a waste of time and energy!

Tom: And it aggravates and increases the severity of the cancer! My illness has been pretty straight forward. I knew from the beginning that I would die of this incurable thing if the Lord didn't intervene. I haven't had any major setbacks along the way, just a gradual deterioration. I have easy days and not so easy days, but never bad days. I make sure of that. How about you, Mike?

Mike: I was diagnosed in 2005. I started bleeding and having pain in my rear end. I had a history of minor hemorrhoids so I attributed my episodes to that. About ten years earlier, I had fallen and landed on the corner of a wooden stair, breaking my coccyx bone. Time and again, it would hurt me a lot and then go away. I attributed this pain to that existing problem.

Tom: Several good reasons to procrastinate about going to a doctor.

Mike: That's what I thought! Like you, I was only too ready to put it off, but I'm not a complete nut! It didn't take me long to figure out I had a tumor and where the tumor was because it was right inside of me and large. I knew I was in trouble and the solution wouldn't be simple. What prompted me to finally go to the doctor was a big episode. I knew then I had to either tweet or get off the twig. I contacted a urologist, a church friend, and had a colonoscopy the next day. I call that my unexpected blessing #1: Having a urologist who took action immediately. After receiving the test results, I called a physician friend in Boston and told him I had a tumor in my anus. He asked if I could be in his office at 11 the next morning. I said, "Yes, sir," and Patsy and I were on a plane and in his office right on time. That's unexpected blessing #2: Knowing one of the best doctors in the world. My friend in Boston is a nephrologist, a doctor who specializes in treating kidney problems. He had taken great interest in me because I had one kidney removed in 1969 when I was 18. We had spent a week together in Hawaii on a business trip in the '90s and had become good friends, even riding bikes together down the side of a dormant volcano. While we were in his office, he called "one of the best surgeons in Boston" (his words), a tall Jewish guy who did over 1000 surgeries a year! That's unexpected blessing #3: Being sent to one of the best surgeons in the world. The surgeon said I should go to his empty office, turn on the lights, sit in his waiting room, and he would see me between surgeries. He eventually came and said, "Your doctor says this is pretty important, but I have a couple of problems. I don't have any nurses on staff today, and I have a guy up there waiting for me to cut him." I said, "Ok, how are we going to solve those problems?" He looked at Patsy and said, "Are you squeamish?" She said, "No, I was raised on a farm." He said, "Good because we're going to take out a piece of the tumor right now." He got out a surgery kit and told Patsy what to do. He had me lower my trousers and get on the table. He told me he didn't have time to fool with an anesthetic so I'd better grit my teeth. He reached in, grabbed a piece of the tumor, and tore it off. He told Patsy to hold the bottle for it and in there it went. As you can guess, that's unexpected blessing #4: An immediate biopsy of the tumor.

Tom: Did it bother you much?

Mike: You better believe it! Agonizing pain! I'm surprised I didn't break some teeth I was gritting so hard! He packed me and said, "That's all I can do now. It's definitely cancer, and you're definitely going to have to have an APR surgery (abdominoperineal resection)." Basically, that involves removing the anus, rectum, and sigmoid colon and getting a permanent colostomy. They staged it as stage 2 cancer and said it was about the size of my thumb. It hadn't perforated the rectum and so was encapsulated in the organ. They thought they could get rid of it with surgery.

Tom: Mine was stage four because it *had* perforated the capsule of the prostate gland and was already in some lymph nodes. That's why the doctors weren't optimistic. Taking out the lymph nodes wasn't an option because the cancer would have just popped up somewhere else. Advanced prostate cancer is like an invisible kamikaze, poised to attack at the first whiff of testosterone.

Mike: My cancer wasn't at all invisible! It was right there, ready to be removed. Everyone had a high level of hope that it could be completely taken out with a knife. Patsy and I went home to Georgia to have Thanksgiving with my brother and the rest of the family while we waited for the surgery.

Tom: Your version of a cruise.

Mike: It was indeed. We had ten days to relax and be with family before the big event. During that time, a friend in Boston who was about to travel to Hawaii for a month's vacation invited us to stay in his house for the entire time we needed to be in Boston. He had a hospital bed brought in as well as other items that were a great help. He even had two people on staff there to help us! That's unexpected blessing #5: Having a thoughtful friend with perfect accommodations for my situation. My daughter Cindy, who is a nurse, flew up to Boston and stayed with us. Unexpected blessing #6: Having a daughter who could care for me—and was eager to do so. I had to pay for the hospital stay out of my pocket, and a room at Mass. General Hospital was over $5000 a day, so the surgeon and my doctor friend concocted a plan. "You have a nurse, a hospital bed, and more than three people to care for you. You do not need to be in the hospital long. We'll schedule this surgery so that you are admitted right after midnight. We won't let you stay more than two days." Unexpected blessing #7 was a big one: Not having to go further into debt. A huge blessing!

Tom: Ordinarily, you would have been in the hospital five to seven days after major surgery like that.

Mike: And have gained at least $25,000 to $35,000 in debt just for the room. God covered every one of my needs. They took me into surgery at four in the afternoon and didn't take me out of recovery to admit me to the hospital until after midnight, thus beginning my first day in my hospital room as early in the morning as possible. That day, when the charge nurse was told I would be released so much sooner than usual, she went ballistic. However, when she saw my doctor friend, she just closed her mouth. After they left, she asked, "How in the world do you know *him*?" I told her he was a friend from outside the medical world. She said, "You have one of the best doctors there is, but I don't agree with what he is doing." In spite of her misgivings, she spent a great deal of time with Cindy, explaining my care and loading her up with necessary supplies. They discharged me at eleven on the second night. Traveling was tough, but we got back to our friend's house and stayed there for 2 ½ weeks. Then, we went back to Georgia. The nurse in Albany who assisted with the removal of the stitches said, "You are probably one of those stubborn guys. You started bleeding, and you ignored it. You started hurting, and you ignored it. Now here you are." I laughed and said, "You're right." I couldn't sit down for over 4 months and was out of work for 7 months. A big price to pay for my pigheadedness!

Tom: Definitely different from my experience. I went back to work within days of my much less serious surgery. I did have to cut back some because of fatigue, though. In fact, I ended up retiring earlier than I expected because of increasing problems handling the rigors of my practice. Soon after I was diagnosed, I had a meeting with my staff to inform them of my condition and the limitations it might place on our work. That meeting sticks in my memory because I had loyal staff members, ladies I appreciated a lot. I told them the diagnosis and prognosis matter of factly, just as I would have told them about any change in the practice. I walked down the hall several minutes later, and they were huddled in an exam room. Several were crying. I remember trying to help them understand that my life wasn't over. I quoted Paul in Philippians. *To live is Christ and to die is gain.* I assured them that though we would have to make changes, life would go on and be as good as it always had been, probably even better. I remember being relieved that my first public response to my cancer was to rest in Christ. The fact that I had passed the test of telling my staff by using Scripture gave me confidence. I thought, "Learning God's Word and trusting Him really works. God is as faithful as He promises." Others—even Christians—might freak out or go into depression, but because of my training in God's Word, making it the priority of my life, I had God's strength to face this crisis with confidence and peace. I realized that even though I wasn't a spiritual giant and had never applied myself to the Bible as I should have, God remained faithful and allowed me to accept my death sentence calmly.

Mike: That had to be exciting for you, realizing the extent of God's faithfulness. I know it was for me.

Tom: And realizing the power of His Word. I believed what God said in His Word so I *knew* I had *nothing* to fear. Throughout this whole cancer experience, you and I have enjoyed the peace that passes all understanding. I wish I had words to explain that peace because it's so remarkable. I don't think we could have had that privilege if God hadn't put us through this cancer test. That's one reason I praise God for allowing me to have this cancer.

Mike: I thank Him every day for making His grace so abundantly visible to Patsy and me. From the moment I realized I had a serious tumor and throughout all my trials, I have been relaxed. Like you, never once have I given in to anxiety or fear. That sure sounds like bragging, doesn't it! But it isn't. The Lord is the One who does it all. I do nothing but sit back and let Him take care of everything. I couldn't have this peace and calm acceptance if I tried to go through this on my own without God. I'd be like a chicken with its head cut off—running around accomplishing nothing and making a major mess of everything!

Tom: God is amazing, isn't He! Our peace—this overwhelming contentment—can't come from anyone but Him.

Mike: My surgeon says he wishes all his patients were as relaxed as I am. His biggest problem is convincing people to have colostomies. Here, years later, the colostomy is nothing, the least of my problems, another gift from God to make my life easier and possible. My *surgery* initially scared Patsy—understandable considering the invasiveness of it, but she quickly realized that the disease wasn't life *threatening,* just majorly life *changing.* We would never be able to go back to the comfortable, relatively easy lifestyle we had before. She has been a real trouper about the whole thing. The surgeon removed 13 lymph nodes along with the other organs. Because the cancer had been encapsulated in the tumor, they didn't find any cancer cells in the lymph nodes.

Tom: They thought the surgery had completely removed your cancer.

Mike: They did indeed. The decision to do nothing more about my initial cancer was supported by the encapsulation and the biopsies, and I was good with it. However, after two years and three months of thinking I was cancer free, in one of my regular scans, my doctor noticed a problem with two lymph nodes. Those two nodes eventually caused the extensive problems I have now. The average life expectancy for the recurrent form of my cancer is 24 months. Right now, I'm in my 68th month. Even a fool like me can see that God has blessed me far beyond human expectations!

Tom: We know the Truth—God alone determines life and death. Thank God we don't have to stumble around worrying we won't find the right combination of treatments or food or exercise—whatever cure the world advocates at the moment! We can relax and let God handle it. Do what seems sensible after prayer and ignore the rest.

Mike: Before the cancer came back, a number of years had passed during which I had acclimated myself to the physical changes brought on by the initial surgery. Those years of facing my mortality gave me an advantage that I had not had when I was suddenly hit with everything in the beginning. Before that first surgery, I was filled with questions and concerns. A colostomy? I knew that it by itself would bring huge changes for both Patsy and me. Add that to the missing parts of my body... I was in the dark about exactly what problems I would face. I decided to zip my lip, make the best of it, and move on.

Tom: And what did you find?

Mike: Everything went smoothly, better than I'd expected. So glad I didn't waste time worrying! After the recurrence of the cancer, I underwent intensive radiation and chemotherapy that left me in terrible condition. It was an intense year. Then, I had 2 ½ years when regular scans showed nothing growing, including those two pesky lymph nodes. They were active but not growing. I call that my vacation. Then, the doctors noted more lymph node involvement as well as spots on my lungs and pelvis. Eventually, the cancer had advanced enough that they put me on chemo again. I've decided not to take the last available drug for colo-rectal cancer, just approved last year, because at best it increases life by only about five weeks and with bad side effects. Interestingly, no doctor in Albany has told me that I am terminal, but I read a report a month ago in which the doctor said, "Mr. McKinnon knows he is dying of recurrent rectal cancer." Recently, I asked my oncologist for a time frame, and he stated it could be as little as six months or on the outside two years.

Tom: But we are not going to check out next week. I probably shouldn't say that. God is omniscient; I'm not. We could get run over by a car in the morning!

Mike: Or die of bird flu, whatever that is! Tomorrow isn't certain for anyone! From the very get go of the recurrence of my cancer, the doctors told me that all they could do was identify the location and use chemo on it. Like maintaining a forest, cancer has to be slashed, burned, or poisoned. Doctors slash you with the knife, burn you with the radiation, and poison you with the chemotherapy! Of course, your body suffers!

Tom: You know you're getting toward the end when your doctor talks in terms of months, not years, and is excited because you are still up-right at your appointment! I'm reminded of a story in a Mark Hitchcock book. A man went to see his physician and the conversation went something like this. "I have some bad news for you. You don't have long to live. You are at 10." "At ten? Ten what?" "Ten, nine, eight, seven..."

Mike: Guess it depends on how fast God is counting, doesn't it! During the last 5 ½ years while I ran my sign and print shop, doing what I could to keep us afloat financially, my appearance cycled from odd during chemo and radiation, back to normal, and then to odd again. I'd be sick and then well. I'd be bald and then have hair. Right now, I have acne and a burr "haircut". Most people haven't known the specifics, but they sure could see I was going through something major. I have used their curiosity as opportunities to witness to God's grace.

Tom: What went through your head as the disease progressed, and you were offered another treatment? How did you decide if a treatment was worth the side effects?

Mike: I've always said that I'm not ready to die. I'm totally *prepared* to die, 100% prepared. But I consider myself like a mad cat in a corner. I'm going to fight until there's nothing else I can do.

Tom: Why? Especially since the treatments themselves are so debilitating.

Mike: I guess because I'm made that way. I never thought about not doing a treatment until last month when I read that letter from the doctor saying I was dying. In that same letter, he indicated that I had elected to continue chemo. I never even thought about not trying more therapies until this last drug.

Tom: I've found that doctors always put the burden on the patient. "You made the decision. Don't blame me that we're giving you this poison that is destroying the good along with the bad. You said you wanted it!"

Mike: I could have stopped my treatments at any time, but I never thought about doing it. I considered it desirable, even if it only added a few months to my life. The negative part of the treatment, I just took in stride.

Tom: Why do you want to fight dying? For whose sake?

Mike: When you put it that way, I really don't want to fight it.

Tom: But you said you were like a cornered cat.

Mike: I was making the analogy that I am *prepared* to die but not *ready* to die. The completion of that analogy is that I tell people I'm prepared to die, but I'm not giving up until I see my number. Then, I'll know the Lord is ready for me, and I'll be ready to die.

Tom: I don't want to give the impression that I've given up either. I'm definitely more interested in enjoying the time I have left than in adding a few months but feeling lousy because of the treatment. Quality of life over quantity, as the saying goes.

Mike: A cancer patient with a terminal prognosis can easily cross that line. I've made it clear to my doctors that I'm not desperate. I'm not going to take the Steve McQueen route. He went to Mexico, took laetrile until he was orange, and died quickly anyway.

Tom: And I'm not about to drink five gallons of carrot juice every day either!

Mike: It's difficult to decide how much treatment and which treatments because where do I draw the line? You chose to have few treatments, but I'm finishing my eighth one right now.

Tom: Those decisions are part of our testimony, aren't they? We try not to go to either extreme, to trust God regardless.

Mike: That's the best explanation. I don't want to be the nut who flies all over the world frantic for a cure, any cure, or the nut who sits back and says I don't want to do anything.

Tom: I've expressed the same thoughts to my oncologist. After my last therapy (it boosted my immune system), I could tell he wasn't enthusiastic about trying anything else. But other treatments are out there. He explained several of them. He waited for me to say, "We've got to do something!" But I didn't. He seemed relieved.

Mike: When the doctors proposed this current regimen and told me I'd get acne, I said okay. An old man with acne might get stares, but as side effects go, it is an easy one. When my doctor said recently he had another treatment, but it would make me really, really sick, I turned it down.

Tom: That's the way with me. One of the treatments I could do now is new. I'd have to go sixty miles to Nashville and the consequences on the heart are pretty severe. I decided I have better things to do than spend my remaining time in a car and feel worse than I have to.

Mike: It's a tough decision.

Tom: It is, one that merits much prayer. My oncologist told me recently that since my first metastasis was to my bones—my right hip bone to be specific, it will probably stay in the bones and not involve other organs. Knowing that helps me better prepare mentally for coming physical problems. I'm more likely to break a bone than to have trouble breathing. Unless the bone break leads to pneumonia, of course! I'm glad the Lord knows what's in store for me, and I can just relax and let Him handle it. Too many Christians frantically seek to help God find a cure when all He wants is for us to sit back and enjoy the journey He has custom-prepared for our greatest benefit and His glory. The Lord's blessings and mercies are unending. I thank Him— praise Him— that my journey has been smooth and tolerable through His grace and power. I'm confident I'll reach my heavenly destination with equally gracious provisions, regardless of the pain and problems. My Father will pour blessings on me and those I love all along the way.

Mike: All this conversation is doing is making me want to get on down the road! It's making me even more eager to get to the other side!

O LORD, YOU ARE MY GOD. I WILL EXALT YOU. I WILL GIVE THANKS TO YOUR NAME FOR YOU HAVE WORKED WONDERS, PLANS FORMED LONG AGO WITH PERFECT FAITHFULNESS Isaiah 25:1

Chapter 2

You Mean God Is Greater Than This Cancer That Is Destroying My Life?

Our Great and Glorious God

"He [God] *stretches out the north over empty space and hangs the earth on nothing. He wraps up the waters in His clouds, and the cloud does not burst under them. He obscures the face of the full moon and spreads His cloud over it. He has inscribed a circle on the surface of the waters at the boundary of light and darkness. The pillars of heaven tremble and are amazed at His rebuke. He quieted the sea with His power... By His breath the heavens are cleared. His hand has pierced the fleeing serpent. Behold, these are the fringes of His ways, and how faint a word we hear of Him! But His mighty thunder, who can understand?"* Job 26:7-14

Tom: Now that we've covered the gruesome details of our cancers, what next?

Mike: I'd say we begin as the Bible does, with God. *In the beginning, God...²*

Tom: God—Creator, Savior, Redeemer, King of kings and Lord of Lords, the Beginning and End. When something seems insurmount-

---

2 Genesis 1:1

able or impossible, I just compare it to God. Take my biggest problem, this killer cancer, for example. The doctors say it can't be cured. I know I sure can't do anything about it! Looked at that way, things look pretty grim. Then, I compare it to God. He formed my body in the womb[3] and gave me life. Is this cancer too big for Him to control? Foolish thought!

Mike: If I keep my eyes on my problem—misery. If I keep my eyes on God—peace and joy. When God is at the center of our thinking, our thinking is centered.

Tom: Nice way to say it, Mike. Like Job in the verses above, I can't discern the mighty thunder, the deep wisdom of God, but the better I understand His character, the better I am able to rejoice always and give thanks for everything.

Mike: That's the key, isn't it? Realizing that God is God, almighty, gracious, and loving.

Tom: When I'm feeling down, that's what I do—remember who God is. My problems shrink immediately. I can trust Him to lead me to *green pastures*, my mental place of rest.

Mike: Why wouldn't we trust our Father to do what is best for us? What can we do compared to Him? We sure can't *hang the earth on nothing*!

Tom: Remember those ads from years ago of the skinny guy on the beach having sand kicked in his face? We're that ninety-pound weakling flexing our pimple-sized muscles when we forget God and try to solve our problems by ourselves. If God is faithful—and I have ample

---

3   *By You I have been sustained from my birth; You are He who took me from my mother's womb; My praise is continually of You.* Psalm 71:6

evidence in my life that shows He is—then I know, I absolutely know, He will uphold me through both pain and dying. I have *nothing* to fear.[4] Because He is always with me, I won't ever be alone, even in the darkness of a coma at the end. I'm foolish if I dread those last days. I can count on His kindness overflowing to me and those I love no matter the mess we are in. I'm so thankful God is God! I breathe that prayer of thanksgiving often.

Mike: I consider myself fortunate to have learned so much about God long before I got sick. Without knowledge of Him, I couldn't love Him, and if I couldn't love Him, I couldn't truly love others.[5] This whole thing would be even harder on Patsy if that were true! Remembering Him and His love for me helps me have peace no matter what comes my way, including the really strange complications of this illness! Some of them would have embarrassed the heck out of me before. I just laugh about them now. They are such an insignificant part of it all. Thinking of God puts my *momentary light afflictions* in perspective.

Tom: God's compassions are immense, unending. Scripture tells us they *fail not.*[6] Knowing that gives me confidence to face each moment with peace and contentment. I *know* God will not fail me. In fact, He will treat me with love and kindness regardless of *my* failures—just as we treat our own children. After all, He is my Father! Such comfort!

Mike: You and I are part of His plan, Tom, as long as we are alive. Patsy and I studied the Book of Esther recently. The central premise

---

4 *"Do not fear, for I am with you. Do not anxiously look about you, for I am your God. I will strengthen you. Surely I will help you. Surely I will uphold you with My righteous right hand."* Isaiah 41:10

5 *We love because He [God] first loved us.* 1John 4:19

6 *This I recall to my mind; therefore I have hope [absolute confidence]. The LORD'S LOVINGKINDNESSES INDEED NEVER CEASE, FOR HIS COMPASSIONS NEVER FAIL. THEY ARE NEW EVERY MORNING. GREAT IS YOUR FAITHFULNESS.* Lamentations 3:21-23

is God's control of history, His careful planning of every moment of every day—and for every person! I enjoyed the subtleties of Esther. For instance, the king couldn't sleep so he called for his secretary to bring boring records of civil actions for him to read. The one he brought pointed out that Mordecai, a Jew and Esther's uncle, had not been rewarded for saving the king's life. Why couldn't the king go to sleep? Why did he decide to read the records? Why did the secretary bring the very one that recounted Mordecai's actions in saving his life? Why was Mordecai not rewarded at the time of the incident?

Tom: I can just hear someone saying, "What good luck!" Or "What a coincidence!" But we know that God coordinates everything in every life to fulfill His plan. Nothing in this world—or out of it!—happens by chance, luck, or coincidence. Even so, God never forces any of us to do anything. He works His plan around our decisions, our freewill. He lets us be as bad or stupid as we want to be!

Mike: And we all have done some doozies! But we're still here and still trucking. All of those seemingly random acts in Esther were in reality God working behind the scenes to bring about His desired end, to save the entire nation of Israel from slaughter. Like Esther and Mordecai, you and I have little grace blessings popping up all around us.

Tom: Not to mention major explosions of grace, like 17 years of extra life for me.

Mike: Too bad we seldom recognize God's hand behind all those blessings. We don't have the Book of Mike or Tom to reveal them to us! We're going to have to get to the other side before we can see reality clearly. In my life, God wove together all those unexpected blessings 1-8 I mentioned earlier. And I'm sure the actual blessings numbered in the thousands, not just in the eights! I am just too spiritually blind to see them all.

Tom: God never fails to do what is best for us. He is so gracious that He takes even my bad decisions and uses them in His plan—for *my* good! Imagine that degree of multitasking! In fact, I can't imagine it—but I know it for a fact. *We know that God causes all things to work together for good <u>to those who love God</u>, to those who are called according to His purpose.*[7] I have to remind myself to claim the beginning of that verse without ignoring the end. I have to continue learning and obeying all parts of His Word for Him to work all things together for my good. Even this cancer!

Mike: You and I both agree that this cancer has been for our good.

Tom: Pain and nausea sure aren't fun, but putting them in God's hands, letting Him comfort and strengthen us, that brings peace, a blessing more amazing than anything I've enjoyed so far in this life.

Mike: A smile-on-my-face peace! We never have to worry about anything. Anything! What our tomorrow will be, we don't know, but God does. He has always known.[8]

Tom: God is my Father. He cares for me. He has everything under control. What disrespect to Him if I get depressed or start whining! Why is this happening to poor, little me?

---

7   Romans 8:28

8   *And which of you by worrying can add a single hour to his life's span? If then you cannot do even a very little thing, why do you worry about other matters? Consider the lilies, how they grow: they neither toil nor spin; but I tell you, not even Solomon in all his glory clothed himself like one of these. But if God so clothes the grass in the field, which is alive today and tomorrow is thrown into the furnace, how much more will He clothe you? You men of little faith! And do not seek what you will eat and what you will drink, and do not keep worrying. For all these things the nations of the world eagerly seek; but your Father knows that you need these things. But seek His kingdom, and these things will be added to you. Do not be afraid, little flock, for your Father has chosen gladly to give you the kingdom. Luke 12:25-32*

Mike: We sure are expert sorrow and misery makers, aren't we?

Tom: Are we ever! We cause most of our own problems—or at least make them into monsters in our minds.

Mike: Kind of like monsters under the bed when we were kids. I was scared to death to go to the bathroom after dark. The moment my toe touched the ground, I was sure IT would get me!

Tom: God says fear causes us to flee from the wind, thinking it's the enemy. Our illnesses can breed those kinds of problems, fears built on imaginary boogey men under the bed. What a comfort to know that God loves us as much as He loved Esther and Mordecai. He is working everything together not just for us, but also for Nancy and Patsy, for our children and grandchildren, for everyone! God never forgets anyone. We can trust Him because He is God.

Mike: God is perfect so His plan for us—every part of it, including our suffering and death—is perfect. Admittedly, nausea and pain are NOT perfect, but they put us in the place we need to be to acquire His perfect peace and joy.

Tom: God's love for us is much greater than we could ever understand. How could any love be greater than giving His only Son to the agony of dying as a substitute for the sins of His enemies?[9] That's us—His enemies! We are *all* sinners. God is perfect yet He loves us even at our most wretched. Christ suffered punishment for every one of our sins, punishment that should have been ours. That is true love.

Mike: God's grace comes from that unfailing love. He constantly pours His grace on His children, and we have been His children since

---

9 *For if while we were enemies we were reconciled to God through the death of His Son, much more, having been reconciled, we shall be saved by His life.* Romans 5:10

the moment we believed in Jesus Christ as our Savior! We are ben-eficiaries of His love every step of every day in every breath we take, including in this cancer. Since I understand that my every breath is a gift from my Creator, it is hard to look at this terminal illness and say it's not supposed to be. If He provides every breath, He has my welfare in mind when He chooses to cut them off.

Tom: I'm afraid too many believers try to remake God to mirror themselves. They can't imagine a love that always does what is best for others. Their version of God becomes as small and impotent as they are—as all of us are. No wonder they fall apart at the first sign of adversity.

Mike: And go into deep depression or bitter anger against God when faced with death. To me, the overriding element of God's essence is His omniscience. He knows everything. Since He knows everything and is our Creator, He will never lead us down the primrose path. In-stead, He will kindly guide us *through the valley of the shadow of death*, and we *will fear no evil because He is with us.*[10] All we have to do is follow Him. He knows everything! You'd better believe He knows the exact path we should be on for maximum happiness and peace! And my path might come to its end tomorrow.

Tom: I'm happy remembering that God has the perfect power to do all the best for me. I can entrust my family to Him. I don't have to worry or wonder about their futures.

Mike: I saw an interviewer ask Andrea Bocelli, the famous singer, how he was able to handle family, career, the problems of travel, music selection, recording, demands for this and that. She finished (and I paraphrase), "I'm sure all this causes you many problems, especially since you are blind." He replied, "Oh, yes, it causes problems, but I just pray to God and tell him my problems and—poof—they are gone. He

---

10 Psalm 23

handles them for me." She said, "Surely, it's not that easy." He smiled and replied, "Yes, it is."

Tom: Poof and every problem loses its power. What a great way to describe God's care of us! The true problem is that we have to choose to put our lives into His hands. Every part of our lives. And we don't like giving up control.

Mike: I know what you mean, Tom. We want to complicate our problems by trying to fix them ourselves when the Lord just wants us to lay them at His feet and let Him handle them. We're not good at being patient. [11] We want everything done right now—or preferably yesterday. The fast food mentality! But God isn't a genie. He does everything at the right time in the right way. We do what we can do and then get out of the way so He can do everything else.

Tom: Andrea Bocelli can trust God because he knows Him. He has developed faith in Him. He stands still in peace because he *trusts* Him.

Mike: I wrote in the back page of my Bible, "Keep your eyes on God." That's what Andrea Bocelli does. The physical side of life is nothing compared to the spiritual. Trust, faith, dependence: The things most Christians don't want to hear.

Tom: Forgetting yourself and remembering God, relying on Him alone. Christ Himself never emphasized the physical. He healed to prove He was the Messiah, not to rid the world of suffering. He left many unhealed. The lepers who came to Him were terminally ill like we are. Imagine their suffering: Slowly, their hands, feet, even their noses and ears rotted away. Talk about ugly deaths!

---

11 *"Do not fear! Stand by and see the salvation of the LORD WHICH HE WILL ACCOMPLISH FOR YOU."* Exodus 14:13b

Mike: Christ was pressured to leave those outcasts alone, but He cured them so He could teach them and us to look to Him, to trust Him with our lives.

Tom: We can't pray to have faith and expect it to come. Faith isn't a good feeling or an emotional high but thoughts and actions based on knowledge of God's Word and His character.

Mike: An old tight rope walker asked an onlooker if he believed he could walk across the wire to the other side. The guy replied, "Sure." "Then jump on my back and we'll go." The onlooker started backing away. The tight rope walker stared at him and asked, "What's wrong? Don't you have enough faith?" Faith in anyone or anything other than God is foolishness, like jumping on that guy's back and expecting a smooth ride across the Grand Canyon!

Tom: We walk up stairs all the time without giving them a thought because we know they are well made. We have faith in them. Stairs made of Tinker Toys wouldn't take us far! Faith in anyone but Jesus Christ is like trying to climb to heaven on Tinker Toys. It just won't work! Faith is knowing God and trusting what you know.

Mike: When we give God everything in our lives, when we become His servants and depend on Him totally, we have everything, so much more contentment, peace, and joy than we ever could have imagined.

Tom: If someone is dying and decides he wants to put his faith in man's solutions to his problem, he will be frantic and shaking with fear. He'll even think Oprah's ideas make sense! His inner turmoil will increase his physical problems. His illness will actually become worse because of his worry and fear!

Mike: His real problem is between his ears, not in his dying body.

Tom: He can't have joy and peace—contentment, either—because his faith is in himself, in being able to find a cure. Until he gives up that futile search—after all, we're all going to die someday— he can't be happy. He can't find shelter under God's wings. Sometimes, I wonder if one of the reasons you and I have stayed alive so long, Mike, is because we haven't worried. Our bodies have avoided the rapid decay that comes—just as God promises—from fear and worry

Mike: And He showers us with joy when we sit back and leave Him in control. God sure isn't my co-pilot. You better believe I want His hands, not mine, on the steering wheel of my life, directing my path!

I shall remember the deeds of the Lord. Surely I will remember Your wonders of old. I will meditate on all Your work *and muse on Your deeds. Your way, O God, is holy. What god is great like our God? You are the God who works wonders. You have made known Your strength among the peoples.* Psalm 77:11-14

Chapter 3

You Mean Heaven Doesn't Have Toilets or Nightlights, and I Won't Need Pain Meds?

Glorious Heaven with our Glorious God

Just as it is written, "Things which eye has not seen and ear has not heard and which have not entered the heart of man, all that God has prepared for those who love Him." 1Corinthians 2:9

Tom: Now that we've established that God is God and we can trust Him to do the best for us even with this killer cancer, I'd say we need to discuss our eternal destination next. Someone who doesn't know how spectacular heaven is sure isn't going to be excited about getting there!

Mike: He needs to understand that God's home is as perfect as God. Patsy and I were listening to a pastor yesterday who said his wife's first cousin's husband and another fellow he knew—both believers—had just died. The day before they had been in severe pain and experiencing high levels of suffering. The report today is that they are just fine. They are in heaven. I like the way he said that.

Tom: I like remembering what God said: *There will no longer be any mourning, or crying, or pain*[12] in heaven. Hard to imagine, especially

---

12 Revelation 21:4

with our present high levels of discomfort! According to Ray Stedman, "For the believer, death is a transition, not a destination. It is a comma, not a period." We don't end when we die. We merely move to a superior place, heaven.

Mike: With superior people. No one in heaven will ever sin. Or even be tempted to sin! Will that be a relief! When Patsy's mother got toward the end of her life (she died at the age of 93), she had huge gatherings at her house with her seven children and their families. She always prayed before the meals, saying something like this, "If everyone in this room could just understand what it is going to be like on the other side. They just don't know, Lord. You just need to make them understand." Afterwards, thinking about it, I realized how right she was. One of my goals, my major goal now, is to put something in this book that will help Christians understand the other side so they won't be fearful of death.

Tom: In fact, they will be excited about being there with their Creator and Savior. I sure am. I know eternity in heaven will be wonderful beyond human comprehension because God promises it, and He is wonderful beyond human comprehension.[13]

Mike: Which is one reason you and I look forward to heaven and don't fear death.

Tom: We are eager to participate in God's eternal life in His actual presence.

Mike: Can you believe I spent over twenty-five years as a student of God's Word without ever really understanding eternity! When I started learning about it about five years ago, I was blown away. It changed

---

13 *Blessed be the God and Father of our Lord Jesus Christ, who has blessed us with every spiritual blessing in the heavenly places in Christ.* Ephesians 1:3

me. An understanding of eternity on the part of a believer who is investing wisely while on this side of eternity will comfort him when he enters the dying phase. Somebody who thinks eternity is merely walking on streets of gold...

Tom: Or playing a harp on a cloud...[14]

Mike: Receives zero comfort. I keep remembering that Jesus has prepared a place for *me*.[15] For Mike McKinnon! The Creator of all the beauty on this earth is the One who prepares heaven for me. No wonder the Holy Spirit doesn't give many details about heaven in the Bible! No words can adequately describe a sunset or a hummingbird's ruby throat, so heaven is certainly beyond mere human words!

Tom: I know I'll be hugely surprised when I go to sleep and wake up in heaven. As Stephen was dying, he saw Christ waiting for him in heaven. Will I see Him, too? I expect to. That's one exciting thought! I imagine that it will be like one of my grandkids going to sleep and waking up the next day to celebrate his birthday. Unmitigated joy!

Mike: Just the fact that time doesn't exist in eternity is difficult for me to grasp. No watches, clocks, or even the rising sun. We won't have any such markers in heaven because time won't exist.

Tom: God created time during the six days of creation—and, yes, the Bible clearly states that those were six literal, twenty-four hour days.

---

14   Revelation 5:8, 15:2

15   *"Do not let your heart be troubled. Believe in God* [God the Father]; *believe also in Me* [Jesus Christ]. *In My Father's house are many dwelling places. If it were not so, I would have told you for I go to prepare a place for you. If I go and prepare a place for you* [and Jesus did], *I will come again and receive you to Myself so that where I am, there you may be also."* John 14:1-3

¹⁶ I'm so glad I understand that. If I based my faith about the past on primordial ooze, a big bang, or some gorilla grandparent, I'd be one confused dude about eternity, too. If God didn't create everything like he said in His Word, then I have no reason to believe He has eternity prepared for me either. How scared and confused I'd be!

Mike: You know, Tom, the bottom line to our eternal existence is subject to whether we believe in Christ not only as Creator but also as Savior. I'm reminded of a story about a poor guy who wasted his life in rotten living. When he died, he couldn't believe he woke up in heaven. His partners in immorality would have been equally shocked. But when he was a tyke, his grandmother had told him about Christ's death for him on the cross, and at that moment he believed in Jesus Christ as his Savior. That moment of simple faith trumped his years of wasted living.

Tom: God's grace is awesome, isn't it? He remains faithful to us even when we spit in His eye so to speak. We go to heaven because at one moment in time we believed in what He did for us, not because of anything we do or don't do afterwards. Thank God my ticket to heaven doesn't depend on me because this ninety-pound weakling couldn't get there on his own even if his life depended on it!

Mike: God knows us too well to make any part of salvation depend on us! I am sad for those who think they will just go to sleep and that is the end, that they won't exist anymore.

Tom: Are they in for a horrible shock when they wake up in Hell. That will be unmitigated horror! *Everyone* who has ever lived will spend eternity in one of two places, either in perfect happiness in heaven or in the absolute agony, despair, and hopelessness of the Lake of Fire. God promises it, and that's another promise He is guaranteed to keep! He

---

16 *By faith we understand that the worlds were prepared by the word of God, so that what is seen was not made out of things which are visible.* Hebrews 11:3

makes sure everyone can be saved if he chooses, but God is a gentle-man. He never forces anyone to go to heaven against his will.

Mike: When they wake up burning in the alternative, they sure will change their minds, but it will be too late. A death-bed conversion does the job, but after death our eternal destinations are locked in.

Tom: Even though most *Christians* believe in the hereafter, if you question them, they know little more than, as mentioned before, the streets are made of gold. The Bible says that is true,[17] but how incon-sequential that is to eternity! God gives us that intriguing detail to stimulate our curiosity, but heaven is so much more. I'm reminded of the story of the rich man who pushed a wheelbarrow full of gold into heaven, ready to pay his way. An angel looked at him in astonishment. "You won't need that here. We already have plenty of paving material!" If heaven's roads are gold, I can't begin to imagine how magnificent the rest of it is![18]

Mike: What will we do in heaven? Most Christians don't know that either.

Tom: They may even think they'll have wings like angels. Is that ever wrong! God made man in His image,[19] higher than angels, so becom-ing an angel in heaven would be a demotion for us. If we have believed in Christ as Savior, we are in God's royal family, for goodness sake! God would never let us be demoted to angels. In fact, He declares we'll rule over angels for all eternity.

---

17   Revelation 21:21

18   The description in Revelation 4 is exciting to imagine.

19   *Then God said, "Let Us make man in Our image, according to Our likeness; and let them rule over the fish of the sea and over the birds of the sky and over the cattle and over all the earth, and over every creeping thing that creeps on the earth." God created man in His own image, in the image of God He created him; male and female He created them.* Genesis 1:26-27

Mike: And we sure won't be sitting on clouds with goofy grins on our faces! Adam and Eve *worked* in the perfect environment of the Garden of Eden, so we should expect to work in the perfect environment of heaven, too; but we won't sweat or grumble. We'll love it. Serving God forever—and always doing it right!—will be glorious.

Tom: If our Creator says that heaven is so great we can't comprehend it, I want to be at the front of the line. That's got to be some kind of great!

Mike: But it doesn't motivate me to leave Patsy.

Tom: I tell Nancy that she'll be jealous because I get to be with our Lord first. I pray that she will get to join me soon.

Mike: That's why you and I are always joking about who will get to have the lowest serial number in heaven. We're looking forward to it. Sometimes, I can't fathom that Jesus Christ will take preeminence over everything, including my wife and children. But that's part of looking forward to heaven. God the Father has designed everything perfectly. We'll love it, and He will be glorified.

Tom: That's the side of the coin that I've depended on the most in looking forward to death. My knowledge of Christ makes me confident that I will be astonished at heaven's perfection. Understanding who He is and what God the Father, Son, and Holy Spirit are as One makes it easy for me to have faith that everything is perfectly prepared and ready for our arrival.

Mike: Flowers on the table and a welcome home cookie at the door! I made that part up, but I know for a fact that Christ has prepared an extraordinary place for us. Every believer should want to enter heaven in a condition of knowledge about it, not in the dark. I emphasize this need for knowledge so much because before I understood as much as I do about eternity—which obviously isn't nearly enough—I was in the dark in many ways. Now, I stay excited, knowing that God has so many blessings waiting for me in eternity. I know it's going to be breathtaking—literally.

Tom: Pastor E.M. Bounds (1835-1913) had a wonderful way with words. His description of heaven and earth sticks in my mind. "Earth is a vast cemetery, and to stay is to live in the graveyard…Here death reigns, imprisons, and ruins. There, life reigns, emancipates, and enriches." Every step I take should remind me of the graveyard of death that confines me here on earth. Heaven is a real place. It's God's home, and He'll soon share it with me. How free of all constraints and restraints I'll be when I live with Him! How can I but rejoice to be free of this decaying graveyard we call earth!

Mike: And to be with our Lord and Savior Jesus Christ! What unimaginable joy!

Blessed be the God and Father of our Lord Jesus Christ, who according to His great mercy has caused us to be born again to a living hope through the resurrection of Jesus Christ from the dead, to obtain an inheritance which is imperishable and undefiled and will not fade away, reserved in heaven for you, who are protected by the power of God through faith for a salvation ready to be revealed in the last time. In this, you greatly rejoice even though now for a little while, if necessary, you have been distressed by various trials so that the proof of your faith, being more precious than gold which is perishable, even though tested by fire, may be found to result in praise and glory and honor at the revelation of Jesus Christ; and though you have not seen Him, you love Him, and though you do not see Him now but believe in Him, you greatly rejoice with joy inexpressible and full of glory, obtaining as the outcome of your faith the salvation of your souls. 1 Peter 1:3-9

Left to right back
Austin, Jacob, Tommy, Robert, Mike
Left to right front: Peyton, Cindy, Lori, Patsy

Chapter 4

Joy, Peace, Contentment, and Thanksgiving While Dying? Your Chemo Has Gone to Your Head!

Rejoice always. Pray without ceasing. In everything give thanks. For this [rejoicing, praying, thanksgiving] *is God's will for you in Christ Jesus.* 1 Thessalonians 5:16-17

Tom: Okay, Mike, we've established that we can trust God to be God (and that's a very good thing!) and that heaven is vastly superior to this chaotic world we call home now, but that doesn't change the fact that we still live here. Now, I think we need to explain why our lives don't have to reflect the world's chaos, how we can be relaxed and happy even with bills and bullying bosses, with nausea and pain.

Mike: How we can have a tiny bit of heaven even though we are still on earth, you mean. I have the habit of telling people that my Bible from Genesis to Revelation tells me to take my eyes off the physical and put them on the spiritual. Then, dying is reduced to just another physical thing that won't last. The spiritual will last forever. Too many people, when they hear they are going to die, go ballistic because, all of a sudden, they don't have control of the physical. I'm thankful that I don't have that fear or feeling of impotence. That would make my pain truly painful!

Tom: It's strange to think back, Mike, and realize you and I weren't changed much by our sudden entrance into the dying phase. That level of mental stability and tranquility has to come from God.

Mike: It certainly can't come from us! It's living in God's plan, the reality of it, every day. Whatever comes along is merely another step in that plan and shouldn't be feared.

Tom: You and I are able to remain calm in what the world thinks is the worst possible tragedy because we know God loves us with a love beyond our comprehension and *always* does what is best for us. So this cancer is for our best. Our spiritual best. Our eternal best.

Mike: Sometimes, we have to suffer physically so we can soar spiritually. My whole life I've enjoyed everything I did. I am in love with life. Even my nine year old grandson Peyton has noticed. He told Patsy recently that he loves being with me because I love life and adventure. That attitude comes from applying God's Word to my life. And I am facing death with the same gusto I've always faced life. I'm determined to squeeze the very best out of every moment I have left.

Tom: You and I have finally learned that happiness does not come from acquiring or doing "things" but from appreciating God and His blessings. I think of Fanny Crosby, the blind hymn writer. Two of my favorite of her hymns are "To God Be the Glory" and "Blessed Assurance." At the age of eight, she wrote,

Oh, what a happy child I am although I cannot see.
I am resolved that in this world contented I will be.
How many blessings I enjoy that other people don't.
To weep and sigh because I'm blind, I cannot and I won't.

She was only eight years old! If that blind child rejoiced in God's grace, surely—to paraphrase her words—I can and will! I absolutely cannot be happy if I'm not content and thankful for *every* blessing God has brought into my life, both those the world applauds as great and those they label as tragic. Every event, thing, person, and, yes, every calamity in my life comes from my loving Father. Note: *Loving* Father. His love never wavers.

Mike: And He continues loving us with the same perfect love no matter how good—or bad!—we are. Amazing grace! When people say to me that they can't believe I'm calm about this cancer thing, I say, "What do you expect me to do? Sit in a corner and suck my thumb." Give me a break!

Tom: Even Christians can resort to that. I'll never forget when one of my staff member's mother became ill. Always before, she had dressed as if she were going to church—jewelry, clothes, hair—a genuine southern lady. Her husband was devoted to her, including during her illness. When she died, suddenly *he* was gone, too, depressed to the point of being bed-ridden. His decline came almost overnight. He totally gave up on life and lived in misery for several years after her death. That to me is an extreme example of "why did God let this happen to me?" So sad and so unnecessary.[20]

Mike: I've learned that being content is the greatest way to live— even now with this messy cancer. I can remember a time or two in our lives when Patsy would get frustrated because nothing bothered me. It bothered her but not me. This cancer has brought her to a high level of contentment, too. She is prepared for everything that will come.

---

20 *But godliness actually is a means of great gain when accompanied by contentment. For we have brought nothing into the world, so we cannot take anything out of it either. If we have food and covering, with these we shall be content.* 1Timothy 6:6-8

Tom: A billboard near us reads, "Discontentment is the thief of joy." A paradox: When we aren't content, we rob ourselves of joy, the very thing we hope to obtain through changing something we don't like in our lives! Ray Stedman wrote, "Joy is a gift of God and it comes to those who take life daily, *whatever it may bring,* from the hand of a loving Father." My *loving* Father is the source of my joy. He won't fail me even in the most awful pain and suffering.

Mike: Without contentment, we can have no joy. And we make everyone around us miserable. One of my greatest joys comes when my contentment and peace spill over to others.[21]

Tom: I like this saying (I don't know who said it first): *I'm always giving the Gospel, but seldom do I use words.* I want my lifestyle to be a light everyone sees, from the checkout girl who's having a bad day to my wife. If I am grumpy (and I sure can be, especially when I'm hungry!), or if I'm whiny, frustrated, or anxious about anything, including my cancer, I live in darkness and bring others down into it with me. When I am content, joyful, at peace, I can see that I raise their spirits, too. The fruit of the Spirit seems to be contagious.[22]

Mike: I think that God's peace is all His gifts rolled up in a nice package. For me, the ultimate peace comes from knowing that I am doing exactly what my Creator wants me to do. That's also the ultimate joy. When I'm focused totally on Christ, the distractions of Satan's world, including the pain, no longer control me. Pain is no longer my master. I think that ability to rest in the Lord is the consummation on earth of everything we've been working toward throughout our spiritual lives.

---

21 *Be anxious for nothing, but in everything by prayer and supplication with thanksgiving let your requests be made known to God, and the peace of God, which surpasses all comprehension, will guard your hearts and your minds in Christ Jesus.* Philippians 4:6-7

22 *But the fruit of the Spirit is love, joy, peace, patience, kindness, goodness, faithfulness, gentleness, self-control.* Galatians 5:22-23

Tom: Resting in the Lord like that is a "Hallelujah Moment" for me. I've finally let go of my feeble attempts to *find* happiness (remember the ninety-pound weakling!) and instead obeyed God's command to focus exclusively on Him and His Word. The happiness I thought I could buy or obtain somehow pales into insignificance compared to the happiness God gives me when I follow Him. Notice the word "follow." If I try to lead God into giving me the things I think are best for me, I make myself miserable! I have to be content to follow Him by obeying His Word and being satisfied with His provision.

Mike: A good slogan: Immerse yourself in God's Word and get peace.[23]

Tom: A *great* slogan! If we depend on God, He absolutely will comfort us in our suffering. You and I, Mike, know for certain that He is with us because we have a peace and contentment beyond anything we could manufacture on our own. And it lasts!

Mike: Even when this pain seems unbearable! No situation, even the depths of pain, is too hard for Him to fill with joy and peace.

Tom: We can tell God the Father our needs—for instance, that we need to stop worrying or complaining. Then, we should relax, stop sinning, and let Him meet our needs.

Mike: If we panic because we know we can't do anything to erase our death sentence, we will spend our precious remaining moments in fear and frustration. We'll make the inevitable dying process horrible. We'll do it to ourselves.

---

23 *In peace I will both lie down and sleep, for You alone, O LORD, MAKE ME TO DWELL IN SAFETY.* Psalm 4:8

Tom: God doesn't want us to be afraid. He promises that we don't have to fear any part of dying, but we will if we worry. He meets our needs primarily through His Word.

Mike: The suffering we go through prior to death plays a big part in bringing us peace. Knowing that, the last thing I want to do is take suffering out of my life. Some friends convinced me to sing in church recently. You'll love the lyrics of the song they chose.

Until Then

My heart can sing when I pause to remember
A heartache here is but a stepping stone;
Along a trail that's winding always upward,
This troubled world is not my final home.

But until then my heart will go on singing,
Until then with joy I'll carry on,
Until the day my eyes behold the city,
Until the day God calls me home.

The things of earth will dim and lose their value
If we recall they're borrowed for a while;
And things of earth that cause the heart to tremble,
Remembered there will only bring a smile.

But until then my heart will go on singing,
Until then with joy I'll carry on,
Until the day my eyes behold the city,
Until the day God calls me home.

Tom: How perfect! We truly are on the upward trail and singing with joy as we go. Even if you never say another word, everyone who heard you sing knows you are confident in your Creator's plan. Clay Ward, my pastor, is teaching 1Peter so we are learning much about joy in suffering. Peter emphasized that we can and should handle our suffering with joy. In fact, God designs suffering to increase our joy and peace! He wants us to trust Him so much that we actually *thank* Him for our suffering. Yes, thank Him for the pain and nausea! That's part of giving thanks for everything. Peter indicated that if we are joyful and at peace in the midst of suffering, we have reached the highest level of spiritual maturity we can attain on earth. Like Peter, James wrote that joy and suffering are compatible.[24] We can and should experience them at the same time.

Mike: God intends for us to *find* great joy *because of* our suffering. He designed suffering to increase our joy. Only God could make that work! You and I both know that the joy we have now is much greater than any we had before. That joy greatly eases our pain and problems.

Tom: The reason we have suffering at all is because we live in a fallen (sinful) world. Adam could sin in only one way, by eating a piece of forbidden fruit. Hard to believe the first sin was eating fruit!

Mike: I have a friend who thinks eating fruit should still be considered a sin. So should eating green vegetables according to him.

Tom: I bet he endorses French fries.

Mike: I heard him mutter something about fruit of the Spirit!

---

24 *Consider it all joy, my brethren, when you encounter various trials, knowing that the testing of your faith produces endurance. And let endurance have its perfect result, so that you may be perfect and complete, lacking in nothing.* James 1:2-4

Tom: We don't know what fruit Adam ate, but I suppose it could have been a potato.

Mike: A *tomato* is a fruit, not a potato!

Tom: Knew that didn't sound right! Regardless, Adam's fruit sin, his rebellion against God, brought suffering into God's perfect world. Since then, everyone has suffered because of sin, our own sins and those of others.

Mike: I've had people ask, "If you have an omnipotent God of perfect love, why does He allow suffering? Why doesn't He stop suffering?" *God* didn't put suffering into His perfect creation. Our forefather Adam did when he decided he didn't have to obey God, that he could and should eat that piece of fruit.[25]

Tom: Adam didn't know that his rebellion would bring super-sized catastrophes onto the earth, but God had warned him. Adam just didn't want to understand. I know I'm his relation because I've sure been bone-headed, too, wanting what I want even when I know it's wrong.

Mike: We all have Adam's sin urges in us, don't we? As God Himself told Cain, we have to learn to master them![26] God certainly didn't create suffering, but He does allow suffering in our lives so that we can grow spiritually and have the mental stability that we would have had automatically if Adam hadn't chosen to sin. Because I understand that, I have great peace. Peace is easy when I'm living my life for the Lord. I

---

25 *Therefore, just as through one man sin entered into the world and death through sin, and so death spread to all men, because all sinned.* Romans 5:12

26 *"If you do well, will not your countenance be lifted up? And if you do not do well, sin is crouching at the door; and its desire is for you, but you must master it."* Genesis 4:7

know He's in control. When I try to rip control from His hands, that's when I go into a tailspin of worry and indecision.

Tom: Worry can't plague us when we walk with Him, depend on Him, trust Him.

Mike: I just sit back, relax, and depend on Him to do the impossible. I know the Lord tests me with suffering for one main reason—because He loves me. I've always expected my road through life to have bumps and the occasional huge crater because God wants me to glorify Him while going through them so I can gain great rewards.[27] That gives me boundless comfort and peace, God's peace, during this crater of all craters.

Tom: Perhaps peace is part of the definition of spiritual maturity. When a believer has God's peace even in tough times, he knows he has reached a higher level in his relationship with God. God is no longer a blurred figure somewhere in the sky, but the Almighty Creator who had him personally in mind as He bore his sins on the cross and who continues to preserve, protect, comfort, and uplift him. That knowledge brings joy, peace, thanksgiving, and the other fruit of the Spirit that make life, including dying, such a glorious journey.

Mike: Sharing the happiness of God, being focused on Christ, and having peace are integrally related. If we have one, we're bound to have the others to a greater or lesser degree. And they are the reason we can smile through all our pain and problems.

Tom: Experiencing so many miracles in our lives, especially during these illnesses, has made you and me much more appreciative of God's greatness, making it easier for us to give thanks. We can more eas-

---

27 *And without faith it is impossible to please Him, for he who comes to God must believe that He is and that He is a rewarder of those who seek Him.* Hebrews 11:6

ily recognize His work in blessing us through our suffering.[28] He was equally faithful and generous when we were healthy, but now His grace leaps out and demands our recognition.

Mike: We live in Satan's world with all its escalating evil, but we can look down the road and know we'll be going home to heaven soon. That's a major reason to give God thanks.

Tom: He *will* deliver us from this *evil age*. We are His ambassadors on earth for only a short time.[29] Soon, He will take us home where we belong—with Him.

Mike: You and I, Tom, are face to face with the ultimate solution to Satan's wicked, chaotic world. We are leaving it and going home!

Tom: I'm so thankful to be this close.

Mike: To almost have this mess behind us. I'm convinced that when we get to the other side, we're going to wonder why we scratched and clawed to stay down here so long!

Tom: I'm thankful for MY cancer, Mike. You can have yours.

Mike: Mine is pretty ugly, isn't it?! But yours is no bed of roses either. We should thank God for every part of our dying process. Scripture

28 *Know, therefore, that the LORD YOUR GOD, HE IS GOD, THE FAITHFUL GOD, WHO KEEPS HIS COVENANT AND HIS LOVINGKINDNESS TO A THOUSANDTH GENERATION <u>with those who love Him and keep His commandments</u>.* Deuteronomy 7:9

29 *For our citizenship is in heaven, from which also we eagerly wait for a Savior, the Lord Jesus Christ; who will transform the body of our humble state into conformity with the body of His glory by the exertion of the power that He has even to subject all things to Himself.* Philippians 3:20-21

says to give thanks for everything, not just the "good" things. Everything—we all have to work on that kind of thanksgiving.

Tom: Thankfully, God the Holy Spirit gives us the power to be grateful for even the most difficult times. We couldn't begin to do that on our own. But God expects us to. That's His will for us. Why? Because then we glorify Him, and He can give us the rewards He has waiting for us in heaven. God always does what is best for us. I say that a lot, but that comforts me more than just about anything. God loves us and always gives us, His precious children, the very best.

The law of the LORD [Scripture] *is perfect, restoring the soul. The testimony of the LORD* [Scripture] *is sure, making wise the simple. The precepts of the LORD* [Scripture] *are right, rejoicing the heart. The commandment of the LORD* [Scripture] *is pure, enlightening the eyes. The fear of the LORD* [Scripture] *is clean, enduring forever. The judgments of the LORD* [Scripture] *are true; they are righteous altogether. They are more desirable than gold, yes, than much fine gold, sweeter also than honey and the drippings of the honeycomb. Moreover, by them Your servant is warned. In keeping them there is great reward.* Psalm 19:7-11

Left to right: Jacob, Mike, Peyton, Austin

Chapter 5

You Can't Mean That God Has Work for Me to Do Even While I'm in Line to Push Up Daisies!

Heavenly Rewards

"Behold, I [Jesus Christ] *am coming quickly, and My reward is with Me to render to every man according to what he has done. I am the Alpha and the Omega, the first and the last, the beginning and the end. Blessed are those who wash their robes* [confess their sins], *so that they may have the right to the tree of life and may enter by the gates into the city."*

~ Revelation 22:12-14

Tom: While we all relish being filled with peace and joy on earth (It sure makes our struggles easier!), we need to explain that our great God has bigger plans in mind for us. The benefits we enjoy on earth when we put our problems in God's hands bring even greater benefits to us in eternity!

Mike: Here we are on earth working to carry out all of God's commands. Why? Because Jesus is *coming quickly*! He could come back for us at any moment, even the next moment. We'd better be prepared because when He does, He'll judge us. That's right—He will judge the worth of everything we've done on earth. He will reward us according to the way we lived our spiritual lives on earth.

Tom: "Tom Northcott, you spent a total of three years one hundred twenty days and 33 minutes being frustrated, this much time wishing for what you didn't have, this much thinking about sports, this much watching TV, this much reading books, this reading the Bible while filled with the Holy Spirit, this praying, this telling others of My gift of salvation…" Of course, I don't know exactly what He will say, but I'm afraid a lot of it won't reflect well on me.

Mike: When you say it like that, I feel a little trepidation. I've wasted plenty of time, too.

Tom: And been motivated by too many wrong things—the praise of others, a business advantage, an "important" position. My missing rewards in heaven will reflect it. Knowing my many failures, I'm even more thankful for the rewards God has already given me—peace, joy, contentment, my family—blessings much beyond my pitiful worth.

Mike: And He has so much more available for us eternally. Especially, He wants us to merit reigning with Christ for all eternity. We can rule with Him in the Millennium and then forever. What a motivation that is to serve Him now!

Tom: Our generous God has reserved for you, for me, for all believers actual, tangible, lasting, valuable rewards! They are just waiting in heaven for us to earn by serving Him faithfully while on earth. Of course, I don't have the power or ability to earn anything worthwhile. I can please God and earn eternal rewards only through relying on the Holy Spirit's power and provisions, only through obeying God's Word.

Mike: I keep reminding myself that I lose rewards every time I don't obey God. What I do now *will* determine my rewards, which will determine my responsibilities in eternity. Ruling with Christ is my goal! I have to obey God in everything—at least as much as possible—and there I'll be, scepter in hand. The Holy Spirit is the One who will make it possible. If I allow Him to rule my life, I'll gain that reward—and others.

Tom: Let's set the record straight though—everyone will have perfect happiness in heaven regardless of his authority or rewards. Today, people focus on inequality on earth. Are they ever wrong! We have total equality on earth because everyone can believe in Christ as Savior, and every believer can earn his rewards. On earth, God doesn't allow anyone to have less access to either. BUT—and this is a big but—in heaven we will have total inequality. God will rank us and reward us based on the spiritual quality of our lives on earth. Everyone in heaven will be able to see if I was God's enemy or servant while on earth—and how much time I spent being each!

Mike: Like wearing a neon sign: Mike McKinnon wasted too much of his life, but he sure enjoyed his dying! He maxed out in the end.

Tom: It may not be neon but close to it. We'll have varying degrees of light depending on how strongly we reflected God's light on earth.[30] God tells us about His rewards to motivate us. He uses them to lead us to the greatest motivation, the desire to glorify Him in everything. Rewards are the carrot in front of a stubborn mule. That mule is me!

Mike: As a pastor friend says, "We are all slug slime." In your case, mule droppings. Ha! Ha! We are worthless without God. He's the one who gives us the ability, power, and provision to glorify Him and gain His rewards. We owe everything to Him. I don't look at myself as serving God for rewards either. I look at myself as serving God as His faithful servant. What Christ bestows on me in heaven is His prerogative. He has treated me magnificently on earth, and I expect no less in eternity.

---

30 *Those who have insight will shine brightly like the brightness of the expanse of heaven, and those who lead the many to righteousness, like the stars forever and ever.* Daniel 12.3

Tom: Without doubt, knowing that God has chosen gifts especially for me makes me want to obey Him, to live my life for Him, so that I can unwrap them in heaven. He is the Great Gift Giver after all! What unimaginable joy we will have as we receive those rewards because they will mean we pleased Him during our lives on earth!

Mike: In heaven, when we receive our rewards, we will be compared with our perfect Creator, not with each other. Did we live as He lived, love as He loved? We won't have egos, but we will have distinctions in rank and rewards. Some believers will receive the Overcomer rewards that Christ revealed to the Apostle John in Revelation 2-3. Some will have less responsible jobs, but no one will be dissatisfied because no one will have the Sin Nature that harassed him on earth. Let's repeat that—you and I are determining our eternal responsibilities right now by our obedience to God and His Word.[31] I feel like I should magic marker that on my brain!

Tom: I shudder to think that I could be one of those believers who will feel shame at Christ's judgment because I didn't obey God at the end of my life. If the Apostle Paul feared losing rewards and not reaching the prize, I'd sure better guard my thinking from the temptations of the world because Paul knew God's Word way better than I do! Even this close to the end, I could stop trusting God and enter heaven bankrupt. The Lord knows my true thoughts and motivations so I can't fool Him. He'll judge me fairly, for better or worse. I'd better stay focused on the better![32]

---

31 *Then all the trees of the forest will sing for joy before the LORD, FOR HE IS COMING, FOR HE IS COMING TO JUDGE THE EARTH. HE WILL JUDGE THE WORLD IN RIGHTEOUSNESS AND THE PEOPLES IN HIS FAITHFULNESS.* Psalm 96:12b-13

32 *Finally, brethren, whatever is true, whatever is honorable, whatever is right, whatever is pure, whatever is lovely, whatever is of good repute, if there is any excellence and if anything worthy of praise, dwell on these things.* Philippians 4:8

Mike: The way I look at it, our respective cancers give us remarkable opportunities to carry out God's will by displaying lives of peace and joy. I've been asked why I'm not spending my time fulfilling a bucket list of earthly pleasures and experiences. In fact, that is exactly what I am doing. My bucket list for my remaining time is to please God. That's it.

Tom: Before I was diagnosed, I often thought that all I wanted was to get to heaven, that once there I would be satisfied just being a sweeper of those heavenly streets of gold. I've concluded that my attitude was self-serving, not God-serving. I had fallen into the dangerous rationalization that God didn't want much of me because I had done the greatest thing by believing in Christ as my Savior. I could just put myself on autopilot and coast into heaven by continuing to live life on my terms. If I were nice to everyone and worked hard, I'd be all right.

Mike: In other words, you were a complacent, biblically lazy fool! Sadly, most of us are just that, more eager to please ourselves and others than to please our Creator.

Tom: Facing death has changed my attitude dramatically. Now I know that just being in heaven won't be enough. Serving God is my goal now. That new way of thinking helped me get past the idea that "If I'm going to die, let's get it over with, the sooner the better. I'm tired of this pain and suffering." I have concluded that as long as I am on this earth, the Lord has a reason for me to be here. The best I can comprehend, that reason is for me to prepare myself to serve and glorify Him to the max on this earth so that I can also serve and glorify Him to the max once I am with Him in heaven.

Mike: As I have grown spiritually, my motivation to look forward to eternity has changed from a desire for rewards to an intense, overriding yearning to glorify God in *everything* I think, say, and do— another impossibility if I don't have the power of the Holy Spirit behind me.

Tom: Maybe God in His sense of humor will make me a street sweeper since that was my goal for so many years. If so, that menial job will reflect Christ's evaluation of my life on earth. Did I thirst to know His Word? Did I sacrifice the materialism and "fun" of the world to serve Him?[33] Did I obey Him in *everything*? Was my thinking in line with His thinking in the Bible? Did I actively care for fellow believers, spend my money wisely for His glory, control my sinful lusts, tell others about Christ boldly and often? Was I His faithful servant in every part of my life? Every part—that's tough. Warren Wiersbe wrote, "The person who cultivates integrity realizes that there can be no division between 'secular and sacred' in the Christian life; *everything* must be done to the glory of God. 1Corinthians 10:31." (*Whether, then, you eat or drink or whatever you do, do all to the glory of God.*) That's my grandson Jonathan's current favorite verse. I hope he continues to hold it dear throughout his life. His happiness will be glorious to behold if he does!

Mike: Eating and drinking are pretty mundane, but we should do even those simple things in a way we know will please God because the degree to which we submit our wills to God's will determines the degree to which we will reflect God's glory in heaven.

Tom: And we can submit to God only if we name every known sin to God the Father and consistently *grow in the grace and knowledge of the Lord Jesus Christ.*[34] God makes serving Him easy because we use His power, His Spirit. We just have to choose to *do* it!

Mike: If we succeed in relying on God, He will give us those re-

---

33   *But whatever things were gain to me, those things I have counted as loss for the sake of Christ. More than that, I count all things to be loss in view of the surpassing value of knowing Christ Jesus my Lord, for whom I have suffered the loss of all things, and count them but rubbish so that I may gain Christ and may be found in Him...* Philippians 3:7-9

34   2Peter 3:18

wards He has waiting for us in heaven.[35] Those believers whose lights shined brightest on earth will receive crowns![36] I think this old bald head would look quite good in a tiara, don't you?!

Tom: That's a picture that will be hard to get out of my mind! The fact that the Holy Spirit expends so much ink on rewards lets us know how important it is to Him that we devote our energies and time to glorifying Him through the power of the Holy Spirit.

Mike: I pray every morning that every step I take will bring glory and honor to Christ, which will be transferred to the Father. I've thought about the archangels in relation to the cherubs and the rank and file angels and wondered what they did to get their higher level of authority. Did God create them that way, or did they earn their authority? I would a whole lot rather be the Archangel Michael in eternity, carrying out major duties in God's very presence, than be a lowly angel! I hasten to add that being a lowly saint in heaven, chopping cotton on someone else's plantation, won't bother me, not because I will be relieved to have made it to heaven by the hair of my chinny-chin-chin but because I know that my position is what I deserve. Christ chose it for me, and He judges righteously.

Tom: The other day when Katie and Sam were visiting, we got out a 1000 piece jigsaw puzzle. We looked at all those tiny pieces that were almost the same and concluded that no matter which piece it is, the picture is incomplete without it. Each of us is an important piece in God's plan. No matter our responsibilities in heaven, the Lord will use us in the way that best serves and glorifies Him.

---

35 A few: Psalm 58:11, 62:12, Luke 19:11-27, 1Corinthians 3:8, 14, Hebrews 10:35-36, Revelation 2:23, 11:18, 22:12.

36 The incorruptible crown, 1Corinthians 9:24-27; crown of life, James 1:12, Revelation 2:10; crown of rejoicing, 1Thessalonians 2:19; crown of righteous, 2Timothy 4:8; crown of glory, 1Peter 5:1-4

Mike: Each believer is important to Him because we are His precious children, but we are much more of service to Him if we die spiritually overworked rather than spiritually destitute. We have to grow and keep growing in our understanding of God and His Word and use that knowledge to help others, give the Gospel, work in the church, and all the other good works God commands of us. For the first time in my entire adult life, I have time. The problem is that my time is running out. I know how I feel today, and I know how I felt four weeks ago, and I know my giddy-up is about gone.

Tom: Last year this time, I was bush hogging and chopping firewood for hours at a time, doing the stupid stuff I like doing. Now, God has me on a couch, studying His Word and loving it. I'd enjoy taking the grandkids hunting or revisiting the Creation Museum with them. Instead, they come visit me, and we have a great time just being together. I love having baby Lydia fall asleep on my chest while I doze with her, especially with a fire blazing in our wood stove. And to think my rewards in heaven could be better than that!

This is the day which the LORD HAS MADE. LET US REJOICE AND BE GLAD IN IT. Psalm 118:24

Chapter 6

What, Me Afraid!?

No Need to Fear Either Dying or Death

For we know that if the earthly tent which is our house is torn down, we have a building from God, a house not made with hands, eternal in the heavens. For indeed in this house we groan, longing to be clothed with our dwelling from heaven, inasmuch as we, having put it on, will not be found naked. For indeed while we are in this tent, we groan, being burdened because we do not want to be unclothed but to be clothed so that what is mortal will be swallowed up by life. Now He who prepared us for this very purpose is God, who gave to us the Spirit as a pledge. 2Corinthians 5:1-8

Mike: Even knowing that God loves us and wants only the best for us, even knowing that heaven will be glorious, fear and worry can sneak in and undermine our best intentions. Let's talk about that threat to our joy and peace now.

Tom: Believing 2Corinthians 5:1-8 [above] has helped me insulate my mind from fear and worry. In explaining this passage, Pastor Warren Wiersbe wrote in <u>Be Joyful</u>, "Death had no terrors for Paul.[37] It simply meant departing. This Greek word [for torn down] was used by the soldiers. It meant 'to take down your tent and move on.' What a

---

37 Paul was the Apostle who wrote Corinthians and many of the epistles in the New Testament.

picture of Christian death! The 'tent' we live in is taken down at death, and the spirit goes home to be with Christ in heaven. 2Corinthians 5:1-8. The sailors also used this word. It meant 'to loosen a ship and set sail.' Departure was also a political term. It described the setting free of a prisoner. God's people are in bondage because of the limitations of the body and the temptations of the flesh, but death will free them or they will be freed at the return of Christ (Romans 8:18-23) if that should come first. And finally, departure was a word used by farmers. It meant to 'unyoke the oxen.' Paul had taken Christ's yoke, which is an easy yoke to bear, but how many burdens he carried in his ministry! To depart to be with Christ would mean laying aside the burdens, his earthly work completed. No matter how you look at it, nothing can steal a man's joy if he possesses the single mind 'for to me to live is Christ and to die is gain.'"

Mike: I had no idea this word had so many nuances in the original Greek, all of them helpful in keeping me from worrying about death. I like the idea that I'll feel like a prisoner set free from the confines of this sinful world. As Ronald Reagan said so memorably after the space shuttle Challenger disaster, I'll be glad to have slipped "the surly bonds of earth to touch the face of God!"

Tom: A comforting image, isn't it? I'm helped by remembering that my body is merely a tent, a temporary dwelling until I go to heaven. A seam gets a little loose and then looser. I go to the doctor and try to fix it, but a split begins in spite of the "wonders" of medicine. The door flap starts coming loose, the fabric gets thin in places, and a few stakes have been lost along the way. My body just isn't the same as it was forty years ago. It's even a whole lot more threadbare than it was one year ago! One month ago! Our decaying bodies are God's most vivid reminder of our mortality. "Wake up, Tom," He seems to urge me with every new ache and twinge of pain. "You're going to leave your tent soon! Prepare to meet your Maker!"

Mike: But we sure can be afraid to let go of that old, beat up tent, can't we? I'm exposed to so many Christians who profess belief in eternity but are scared to death of dying. The question is what motivates their fear?

Tom: The Bible says we are slaves to fear about death if we don't believe in Christ.[38] That's easy to see in unbelievers because they have no hope. They are relying on themselves, and all of us know deep down that we aren't worth much. But believers! How can they be afraid that their Savior won't be faithful to shelter them as they die?! That unbelief is sad!

Mike: I think that one cause of fear for most believers is that they are so darn ignorant of God's Word they don't know what to expect after death. They fear what to them is the unknown. The only way to overcome fear of this unknown is to learn about it! And that learning should occur before the "death bed"! After a believer learns what comes after physical death, he cannot help but be excited about experiencing it—whether his own physical death is right around the corner or years away. Way too much great stuff awaits us in heaven for us not to be excited about it!

Tom: No one can look forward to meeting his Savior if he hasn't spent time getting to know Him. God knows everything about us, our every thought and motivation, but how many of us study His Word so much that He becomes our familiar and constant companion?

Mike: The fear of death may not be as hard for some as the fear of pain while dying.

Tom: I sure don't look forward to increasing pain! Who would! Even

---

38 *Therefore, since the children share in flesh and blood, He Himself likewise also partook of the same, that through death He might render powerless him who had the power of death, that is, the devil, and might free those who through fear of death were subject to slavery all their lives. Hebrews 2:14-15*

so, I don't fear it. I handle both pain and fear in the same way, by putting them in God's hands and sitting back and waiting for His solution.

Mike: That's always the best way, isn't it, Tom? To put every problem in His hands and heave a big sigh of relief, knowing He will take care of everything!

Tom: The way He does it intrigues me. Will it be through a Scripture I read or remember, in a message from my pastor, in the words of a friend? Suddenly, I realize the answer! I know what to do or think. Jesus promised, *"Lo, I am with you always, even to the end of the age."*[39] If we fear, we've forgotten Who will never leave us as we *walk through the valley of the shadow of death.*[40] If we remember God is with us, we walk. We don't run scared!

Mike: One reason a believer may reach death and not be prepared is because he has focused too much on trying to *help* God, rather than on trying to *please* God by obeying Him. If believers are trying to do things for God rather than allowing Him to use them, they absolutely won't be prepared to face death. God is God. He doesn't need our help for anything; however, He graciously allows us to use His power to please Him through obedience to Him.

Tom: So that's one answer to the question, "Why don't we fear death?" We have prepared for it through studying God's Word and avoiding wasting too much time focusing on the distractions of life.

Mike: The solution to every problem is simple. God put them in His Word. We just need to get it through our thick noggins that we have to read, study, and memorize every bit of information God has given

---

39 Matthew 28:20b

40 Nancy's stepmother loved hearing us recite Psalm 23 during her last weeks.

us. We need to use that divine knowledge in every thought, action, and word.

Tom: We must keep our eyes fixed on our Savior, not on ourselves or on our pain or on leaving loved ones behind or on any of the other thoughts that bring fear and despair.

Mike: Satan's fiery darts! He sends so many of them our way. He knows just which will most powerfully tempt us to falter, to stop trusting God, to be unhappy, not joyous.

Tom: If we follow God's plan before death pounds on our life door, dying won't be any more traumatic than having the cat die. Unless we have an unhealthy attitude toward cats, of course!

Mike: After all, the last I heard, the death rate among human beings is 100%. Why fear it?

Who will separate us from the love of Christ? Will tribulation or distress or persecution or famine or nakedness or peril or sword?... But in all these things we overwhelmingly conquer through Him who loved us. For I am convinced that neither death nor life nor angels nor principalities nor things present nor things to come nor powers nor height nor depth nor any other created thing will be able to separate us from the love of God, which is in Christ Jesus our Lord. Romans 8:35, 37-39

McKinnon Family

Chapter 7

Answering the Age Old Question: How Can I Become Joyified?

Knowing and Believing God's Word

For the word of God is living and active and sharper than any two-edged sword, and piercing as far as the division of soul and spirit, of both joints and marrow, and able to judge the thoughts and intentions of the heart. Hebrews 4:12

Tom: As we keep saying, knowledge of the Bible is key to facing dying with a smile. Joy, peace, contentment, all come from knowing God as God. That knowledge abolishes fear and worry.

Mike: That's why my best advice for someone facing a death sentence is to get in the Word or get in it more intensively if he is already studying it. Otherwise, he won't have any weapons to handle dying except the foolishness the world wants everyone to use. Eat this, yoga that, pop this pill, contemplate that, whatever you do don't do this…

Tom: A lot of people are desperate to *find* a miracle, aren't they? But they ignore the only place that can bring them real happiness—the Bible. Our knowledge of God's love and power eases our burden and joyifies (a new word) our load.[41] The starting point for finding joy even

---

41 *Let us hold fast the confession of our hope without wavering, for He who prom-*

while under a death sentence is believing that Jesus Christ on the cross took the punishment for each of our sins and not just for us but for everyone who has ever lived or ever will live. God the Father even punished Him for the sins of the Jewish religious leaders who had Him put on the cross! I try to imagine that depth of love but can't. Of course, a God who loves us that much is patiently waiting to help us through any and all suffering!

Mike: God wants everyone to live in heaven with Him,[42] but we have to know Him before we can believe in Him. Therefore, He makes creation scream of His presence. No one has ever seen any verifiable evidence of evolution, any part-bird-part-animal cavorting in his backyard, because evolution is a false system of faith, a lie to put it bluntly. But everyone has seen the grandeur of the skies: Glittering stars, stunning sunrises, clouds stuffed with refreshing rains, a sun that rises every morning without fail over both good people and bad, a moon that lights the night sky—not enough to disrupt our sleep but enough to light our path.[43]

Tom: We see our hands that can perform feats of extreme dexterity, our eyes that can see both tiny flowers at our feet and mountain peaks in the distance, our feet that not only support us but carry us steadily wherever we go—at least until recently for you and me! As God told Abraham, whether we look down at the endless sand of the earth or up at the panoply of stars in the sky, we see the super-abundance of God's

---

ised is faithful; and let us consider how to stimulate one another to love and good deeds, not forsaking our own assembling together as is the habit of some but encouraging one another, and all the more as you see the day drawing near. Hebrews 10:23-25

42 *This is good and acceptable in the sight of God our Savior, ⁴ who desires all men to be saved and to come to the knowledge of the truth.* 1 Timothy 2:3-4

43 *When I consider Your heavens, the work of Your fingers, the moon and the stars, which You have ordained, what is man that You take thought of him and the son of man that You care for him? Yet You have made him a little lower than God, and You crown him with glory and majesty!* Psalm 8:3-5

love and provision for us.

Mike: God tells us that every person knows that He exists, but most push that knowledge away. They suppress it because they don't want to obey Him.[44] God fills our lives with proof after proof of His existence and desire for us to come to Him, but most turn away from Him instead. God is faithful to us, but too often we choose to ignore Him. We think we can do just fine on our own. And so we fear death and feel miserable. Because I know Christ was resurrected, I am confident that I absolutely will be alive after death. I'm filled with peace, not fear.

Tom: Whether we look back at God's sacrifice for our salvation or look forward to His promises for eternity, we see His great love for us. Right now! This very minute!

Mike: Imagine—Jesus Christ and God the Father indwell each of us believers along with the Holy Spirit, a triple whammy of power and grace! Our potential for joy and peace even in suffering is unlimited.

Tom: I know that part of my job from now on is to prepare my soul for heaven. After all, my soul and spirit are the only things from my life here on earth that will go to heaven. When Jesus Christ judges me, I want Him to find good spiritual stuff in my soul, not just football scores, oral surgery techniques, and the news.

Mike: I'm like you, working hard to make each moment count, especially now that I know my time is running out.

---

44 *For the wrath of God is revealed from heaven against all ungodliness and unrighteousness of men <u>who suppress the truth in unrighteousness</u> because that which is known about God is evident within them; for God made it evident to them. For since the creation of the world, His invisible attributes, His eternal power, and divine nature have been clearly seen, being understood through what has been made so that they are without excuse. Romans 1:18-20*

Tom: Too bad we didn't have that same sense of urgency through-out our lives! My main priority is to listen to my pastor-teacher every time the church doors are open and then study his teachings at home. He's a great teacher because he takes us through entire books verse by verse but also includes applicable verses throughout the Bible. I spend much of each day reading commentaries on the Bible, those that are verse by verse studies. Some of my favorite writers, all of whom were/are pastors, are Ron Merryman (www.merrymanministries.com), E. M. Bounds, Warren Wiersbe, Ray Stedman, Mark Hitchcock, David Jeremiah, and Andrew Murray. They help me think through how to use my Bible knowledge in making decisions throughout each day.[45]

Mike: I stay away from any books that aren't by Bible scholars and don't study large chunks of the Bible. Those books about people coming back from the dead come to mind as some of the worst. If they are dead, they aren't coming back! Almost dead is about as sensible as almost pregnant!

Tom: And many Christians read those books instead of the Bible! Sad!

Mike: I used to sit in my little office at home, working on my computer and listening to jazz. Now, I turn on a Bible class instead. I know some Christians would consider it torture to listen to God's Word so much, but for us, learning about God is pure pleasure. I say us because Patsy has shared this passion with me all along. She has benefited as much as I have. Anyone who studies God's Word will benefit. We've seen our lives changed directly in proportion to the amount of God's Word we have learned. God *expects* His Word to change us!

---

45 *Therefore I urge you, brethren, by the mercies of God, to present your bodies a living and holy sacrifice, acceptable to God, which is your spiritual service of worship. And do not be conformed to this world, but be transformed by the renewing of your mind, so that you may prove what the will of God is, that which is good and acceptable and perfect.* Romans 12:1-2

Tom: Though I mentioned commentaries earlier, reading the Bible is the foundation of my study. There's no question that simply reading the Bible on my own has greatly increased my appreciation of God and His plan for me—and made it possible for me to discern good commentaries from bad, too. Reading the Bible focuses my thinking on the object of my faith, Jesus Christ— not on some Bible teacher I enjoy, not on extra-biblical writings that help clarify my thinking, but on Jesus Christ, *the author and finisher of our faith.*[46] Christians make a huge mistake when they leave their Bibles unread on a shelf. I did for years, and my life reflected that mistake. I'm a slow reader, but reading the Bible in a year is easily achievable and has become easier each year. I know I have a better night's sleep if the last thing I do is read the Bible rather than watch Fox News or Monday Night Football. Nance reads it to me now. The last time, I read it to her. We enjoy sharing that time.

Mike: Early on during the process of growing spiritually, I found reading the Bible difficult. My pastor explains the verses he teaches. So does a commentary. But on my own, I have to depend on what I already know to discern the Truth. However, I've found that the more I study God's Word, the more easily I can ascertain God's meaning. I prefer listening to the Word spoken on CDs because I get much more out of hearing it than reading it.

Tom: Nancy and I do the same thing when we are traveling. We use New King James Version CDs; however, we read and memorize the New American Standard Version.

Mike: We do, too. I had a pastor tell me that a lot of people are going to be accountable after they are dead because they walked around with smartphones in their pockets and never accessed Scripture.

Tom, laughing: Will I be held accountable since I don't have a fancy phone?

---

46 Hebrews 12:2

Mike: I bet you have lots of Bibles in your house! It *is* interesting, though, the amount of Bible knowledge in every language many Christians carry around in their pockets, and they don't even think about it. They could be feasting on God's Word every spare moment!

Tom: Context is everything in understanding God's meaning, the context of the chapter, the book, the entire Bible. We can't rip a verse out of its context and expect to understand it as God intends. I know believers who have taken verses out of context and decided they have to be sinless or close to it or they won't go to heaven.

Mike: They sure have a high opinion of themselves! I'd never make it to heaven if being sinless—or even close to it!—was a prerequisite!

Tom: I am amazed that anyone could live with himself and still believe he is sinless! Thank God that Jesus Christ took care of every aspect of salvation for us. He did it perfectly. We sure can't begin to add any perfection to it! I also know people, smart people in other areas of life, who believe that if they miss a church service and die before going back, they won't go to heaven. They can't tell me where the Bible says that, but they sure live in fear of violating that nonsensical rule.

Mike: This may not be the politically correct thing to say, but they are nuts! Thank God that He knows us so well that He designed salvation so we imperfect sinners do nothing but depend on the sacrifice of our perfect Savior.

Tom: We can't lose our salvation because Jesus did all the work. He's perfect so His work for us is permanent. Once we believe in Jesus, we are God's children forever. We sure can't unadopt ourselves. God holds us firmly and forever in His hands.[47] Talk about being comforted in

---

47 *My sheep hear My* [Jesus'] *voice, and I know them, and they follow Me; and I*

dying! There can be no greater comfort than knowing we *are* going to heaven for sure, and we can't do anything—or not do something—to keep from being with our Lord and Savior forever.

Mike: Thank God He doesn't burden us with do's and don'ts to get into heaven, or we'd all be treading fire and brimstone—not water—for all eternity! It's kind of like someone who leaves his father, going as far away as possible, denying he even has a father, even calling someone else his father. But his DNA, his genes, refute his claim. He will always have the same father. God adopted us when we believed that Jesus died for our sins, and we can't do anything to undo that fact.[48] My Father's assurance that my place in heaven is irrevocable is one reason I have this great joy and peace as I face death from this cancer.

Tom: At some point in this mortality journey, preferably soon after believing in Christ as Savior, our God and Father expects us to start growing spiritually and then continue increasing our spiritual understanding until He takes us home to be with Him forever. I'm excited knowing that I will continue learning God's Word in heaven. I dream of sitting at Christ's feet and learning from my Savior Himself. That's the picture of heaven I hold in my mind.

Mike: Therein lies the "problem" I have now. I can't get enough of God's Word! I fill each day listening to recorded lessons by pastors who teach God's Word accurately—that means literally verse by verse. Don't get me wrong; nothing can replace sitting in a pew, getting face

---

give eternal life to them, and they will never perish; and no one will snatch them out of My hand. My Father, who has given them to Me, is greater than all; and no one is able to snatch them out of the Father's hand. John 10:27-29

48 *For while we were still helpless, at the right time, Christ died for the ungodly. For one will hardly die for a righteous man; though perhaps for the good man someone would dare even to die. But God demonstrates His own love toward us, in that while we were yet sinners, Christ died for us. Much more then, having now been justified by His blood, we shall be saved from the wrath of God [the Lake of Fire] through Him.* Romans 5:6-9

to face teaching from my pastor. But I do get great enjoyment augmenting that with lots of other teaching. Yesterday, during our six hour drive to Tullahoma, Patsy and I listened to four hours of Bible class. What a privilege! I learned things I didn't know and was reminded of doctrines I hadn't considered for a while. I've had people—preachers even—ask if listening to so much Bible teaching isn't a little overload. No! Sports or a novel would be better?! You've got to be kidding! I'm interested in learning as much of God's Word as I can so that when the day comes for me to be transferred to the other side, I can take as much Truth as possible in my soul.

Tom: No one ever overdosed on God's Word, that's for sure! Since we've been married, Nancy and I have exposed ourselves to biblical teaching just about every day, but for a long time, it was almost a religious ritual. We put in the time, but our minds were often on other things. I needed a bashing up side my head with a two-by-four to get my attention!

Mike: If yours was a two by four, mine was a Mack truck! I didn't used to be as motivated as I am now. A death sentence changes everything. Now, I'm hungry to know as much as I can—and willing to make the time for it. That's key.

Tom: Our kids swear that we got them up at five in the morning so they could listen to a Bible lesson before they went to school.[49] I'm glad they remember it that way.

Mike: Our children gathered around the breakfast table. We did devotionals because of time restrictions.

Tom: So far, all our grandchildren have believed in Jesus Christ as

---

49 *Train up a child in the way he should go. Even when he is old, he will not depart from it.* Proverbs 22:6

their Savior by the time they were three years old. Immediately, they were eager to learn about God. For them, the spiritual race to reach God's prize[50] started then. We love hearing Reagan, Hannah, and Abigail walk up to our door singing a Psalm or a bunch of verses they've memorized. We can hear them getting closer through our closed door. They truly *shout joyfully*, one of their favorite Psalms to sing.[51] We can't help grinning. They could give us no more precious gift.

Mike: You must rejoice to know your grandchildren's minds are being filled with God's Word at a young age and not the worthless—but dangerously unrighteous—junk that overloads our society.[52]

Tom: They will have such an advantage when adversities like ours enter their lives. And suffering always comes a-calling eventually. No one is immune to problems, even kids. God wants them to have the joy that comes from depending on Him exclusively.

Mike: I consider life to have a hydraulic effect. A believer's body goes down at the same time that his level of spiritual understanding should be going up. At some point, his body will give out, and he will die. Hopefully, by that time, he will have reached a level of spiritual maturity that allows him to welcome death with open arms.

Tom: Preparing for death has been easier for me because that hydraulic effect started early in my life. I would advise everyone to start early reversing the effects of the fallen world in his thinking. Dying

---

50 *One thing I do: forgetting what lies behind and reaching forward to what lies ahead, I press on toward the goal for the prize of the upward call of God in Christ Jesus.* Philippians 3:13b-14

51 Psalm 100

52 *Be diligent to present yourself approved to God as a workman who does not need to be ashamed, accurately handling the word of truth. But avoid worldly and empty chatter for it will lead to further ungodliness, and their talk will spread like gangrene.* 2 Timothy 2:15 17

with its suffering won't seem insurmountable then. They will be prepared.

Mike: Studying God's Word has to be at the top of our To Do list. It is never too late to learn to love God, to gain His joy and peace, to repair a strained relationship, to die with a smile.

Tom: Even if we wait until near the end of our lives to turn to God, He will gladly fill us with His joy and peace. The Holy Spirit has the power to do that. We just have to immerse ourselves in God's Word until we harness His power and ride it through death into eternity.

Mike: We have to continually learn God's Word so that we are prepared for the next minute. We don't know what gasp-producing surprise that minute may bring. Or the next minute! If we consistently defeat every charge of the mosquito (pesky but minor problems) by using God's Word in our souls to remain calm and happy, then when the elephant charges (the suck-in-your-breath-and-get-the-glazed-look-out-of-your-eyes problems), we will reign victorious over them through Christ.

Tom: One of my lifelong mottos is, "Persistence pays." I used to say it to my staff often. They might say too often! Persistence is as important in doing our job for God as in fulfilling our responsibilities in the world. The more persistent we are in learning in God's Word and obeying it, the more consistently our joy and peace will grow. Persistence seems like a synonym for self-control, which God commands us to use. Another fruit of the Spirit

Mike: A friend told me of a lady who knew she could die at any moment. She drug herself to Bible class even though she was weak and tired. She knew the only thing she would take with her to heaven was in her soul, and she wanted to add one more tidbit of Truth before she went to meet her Savior. She died the next day. I thought that was neat.

Tom: I'd love to be able to go out the same way.

Mike: Like a pastor who says he'd like to die in the pulpit. A shock to the congregation maybe, but great for him! I'm curious. How many years of education did you have after high school?

Tom: Let's see...eleven years, I guess.

Mike: I find it fascinating that even with all your school learning, you don't have an advantage over the rest of us in learning God's Word. Even your grandchildren are able to understand fairly difficult spiritual Truths because the Holy Spirit helps them.

Tom: They don't know a lot of details yet—though probably more than most adult Christians—but basic truths, like details of salvation and the source of sin and death, are already easy for them to explain. God the Holy Spirit makes it possible for everyone to understand His Word. We're all His beloved children after all! But it's hard work, daily hard work that God commands us to continue until death. My children are faithful to teach their children daily, but I don't have the luxury of someone prodding *me*. I have to make myself study, read, and memorize. Self-control again.

Mike: A true story was told to me that proves the point that God makes it possible for everyone to learn the deep principles of His Word. A believer gave his yard man, also a believer, a book to read about the spiritual life. When a friend heard which book he had given him, he was appalled. "Oh, no! That book is one of the most complicated and difficult to understand you could have picked." About three months later, the old fellow came to his employer and said, "That was a real good book. I really enjoyed it. I got a lot out of it, most especially I found out that we've been drinking milk at my church while you guys at your church have been eating pork chops!"

Tom: The meat of the Word! Too few churches today teach the meat, the many biblical principles necessary for spiritual growth. Their congregations are starving! They faint when the mosquito buzzes around their ears, so, of course, they fall apart when that elephant death charges toward them. God makes it clear that we must learn His Word before we can have mental stability and inner tranquility. We can have genuine, lasting happiness only if we know God well, if we rely on His essence and character.[53]

Mike: We've all manufactured moments of happiness on our own, but they soon fade. They are as superficial as the momentary highs of alcohol, food, and drugs. And then comes the crash into genuine *un*happiness! Man's solutions can't begin to compare with God's!

Tom: Thankfully, He is wonderfully generous in sharing those solutions with us through His Word. I've found that when I think God's Word and remember His character, when I base every decision on that, I'm happy; and, as a bonus, wisdom spills over into my handling of everything life throws at me.

Mike: I concur that knowledge of the Bible is necessary to please God and have His happiness, but God attaches warnings to that knowledge. Our faith must be in the One we are learning about, Jesus Christ, not in the masses of knowledge we are so proud to have learned. We have to live His Word, not just store it in our thinking. I keep reminding myself that the only way I can ever expect to gain the strength to endure this dying phase with happiness is through increasing my dependence on Him and His Word.

---

53 *How blessed* [happy] *are those whose way is blameless, who walk in the law of the* LORD *[Scripture].How blessed are those who observe His testimonies* [Scripture]*, who seek Him with all their heart.*[3] *They also do no unrighteousness; they walk in His ways. You have ordained Your precepts* [Scripture]*, that we should keep them diligently. Oh, that my ways may be established to keep Your statutes* [Scripture]*!* Psalm 119:1-5

Tom: And there again we have the reason so many Christians are fearful of dying: Ignorance of God and His Word and an unwillingness to obey what they do know.

Mike: I'm ashamed before my Creator that I've been a miserable failure at memorizing the Bible. I finally put a sign on my desk that reads, "Memorize one Scripture every day." It's difficult, but we need a storehouse of verses much larger than mine. I know memorizing Scripture is important because only God's Word has the power to get me through life's difficulties—especially this terminal cancer—with peace and joy.

Tom: I'm like you, Mike. I should have made memorizing verses part of each day for years. Think of the amount of God's thinking that would be my thinking, waiting to be applied appropriately to every situation! I've been able to overcome fear of death so far without many verses in my head, but I would have a greater level of friendship with God if I'd taken His Word to heart. In spite of my failures, God is gracious and brings appropriate verses to my mind, like, "To live is Christ; to die is gain." Whether that's Philippians 1:17 or 21 or 27, I couldn't tell you for sure.

Mike: Ironically, the most Scripture I ever memorized was in Boy Scouts, getting the religious merit badge. I had to affiliate myself with my pastor to get it, and he had me memorize long passages of New Testament Scripture. Then, I was a spiritual mess from my twentieth to my thirtieth birthday, living life without giving a thought to others or God. I was determined to find happiness my own way—and don't get in my way! When I went back to the Lord and got right with Him, got my life straightened out, those verses from Boy Scouts came back to help me. God the Holy Spirit has amazing power to dredge up biblical knowledge that seems forever buried in some dark basement corner of our minds! Even though I don't know a lot of verses, I try to think according to God's Word. Whether it's a leak under the house or somebody getting mad at me, I've tried to view it through the lens of Scripture.

71

Tom: Nancy teaches long passages of the Bible to our grandkids by singing them. Even two year old Abigail sings them, including whole Psalms. The funny part is that now Nance has to sing them in her head before she can recite them! But she remembers them.

Mike: If you give me a cheater's start, I can recite many verses.

Tom: Like Barney on *The Andy Griffith Show* when he was memorizing the law code and wanted to show off. He told Andy to just give him the first word. *The.* Then the second word. *Officer.* Just give me the next one—until Andy had given him the whole thing. By then his hair was all over the place from running his hands through it, and he was a frustrated mess. No question that memorization is advantageous. I would have benefited greatly if I'd learned more and had it ready for the Holy Spirit to pull up.

Mike: Anyone who says he can't memorize Scripture is trying to rationalize his laziness. I know that's true. And so do you, I'll bet, Tom. God the Holy Spirit urges us to put His Word into our thinking, so, of course, He helps us do it. He doesn't ask us to do anything without giving us everything we need to do it.[54]

Tom: The Holy Spirit is the Teacher who never says the wrong thing, never goes on vacation, never stumbles over the unknown, never gets tired or grouchy or frustrated or surprised. He is with us, guiding, caring, and teaching us every step of our spiritual lives. Then, He comforts and strengthens us as we traverse this dying phase, just as He comforted and strengthened Jesus on the cross in the greatest suffering any man will ever know. Christ promised He would send the Comforter, the Holy Spirit, to us, and He surely

---

54 *And my God will supply all your needs according to His riches in glory in Christ Jesus. Now to our God and Father be the glory forever and ever. Amen.* Philippians 4:19-20

kept His Word![55]

Mike: We often sing "What a Friend We Have in Jesus." We could just as easily sing "What a Friend We Have in the Holy Spirit."

Tom: The Holy Spirit throws bacon and eggs in with those pork chops He gives us in His Word! And His desserts are heavenly!

Mike: Heavenly—I like that! Heaven is the dessert of life, isn't it?!

When this perishable will have put on the imperishable, and this mortal will have put on immortality, then will come about the saying that is written, "DEATH IS SWALLOWED UP IN VICTORY. O DEATH, WHERE IS YOUR VICTORY? O DEATH, WHERE IS YOUR STING?" The sting of death is sin, and the power of sin is the law; but thanks be to God, who gives us the victory through our Lord Jesus Christ. 1Corinthians 15:54-57

---

55 *I will ask the Father, and He will give you another Helper that He may be with you forever; that is the Spirit of truth whom the world cannot receive because it does not see Him or know Him, but you know Him because He abides with you and will be in you.* John 14:16-17

Northcott Family

Chapter 8

You'd Better Listen to Me Cause I'm Dying! I Don't Have Time to Say This Twice!

Being a Witness for God

And He [Jesus] *said to them, "Go into all the world and preach the gospel to all creation."* Mark 16:15

Mike: One advantage we have because we are dying is that people are more likely to listen to us.

Tom: Being happy while suffering gets their attention.

Mike: They just can't figure out why we are so darn happy. Too bad joy in suffering is so uncommon that it is noteworthy! I was just told about a man who learned he was terminally ill and would die within a month. He spent that whole time cursing God. Did his bitterness ever speak loudly to those around him! Hopefully, our smiles send an even more powerful message!

Tom: Maybe later, having seen our tranquil attitude during our suffering, others will be encouraged to relax and have peace in theirs, too.

Mike: And increase their desire to prepare themselves to serve God even as they are dying.

Tom: So many opportunities to tell people about God come from living each moment as He commands, from trusting Him to care for us as He promises so often in His Word. People see us confidently living under our death sentence with its pain and problems, and they want to know how in the world we can do it. Our answer is that we can't but God can—and does! I can see your light, Mike, like a spotlight in the darkness. Others can't help but see the difference between you and *mere man,*[56] those who live and die under their own power, fulfilling their own desires like that poor cursing guy. For both of us, our illnesses have made us better disciples for Christ.[57]

Mike: Definitely. I'm dogmatic about that. One of the biggest benefits of this whole suffering and dying thing is being a more effective witness for Christ.

Tom: Maybe we've discovered a motto for DM2 (www.DM2usa. org), my favorite disciple-making (missionary) organization. "Spreading illness is a good way to make disciples." "Be a better disciple—get sick, really, really sick." "Come back from a mission trip with malaria, and people will listen to you." Don't think that will ever catch on! On a more serious note, being more aware of my blessings has made me more aware of my dependence on God. I want to know Him much better before I meet Him face to face.

---

56 *In God, whose word I praise, in God I have put my trust. I shall not be afraid. What can mere man do to me?* Psalm 56:4

57 *I charge you in the presence of God, who gives life to all things, and of Christ Jesus, who testified the good confession before Pontius Pilate, that you keep the commandment without stain or reproach until the appearing of our Lord Jesus Christ, which He will bring about at the proper time—He who is the blessed and only Sovereign, the King of kings and Lord of lords, who alone possesses immortality and dwells in unapproachable light, whom no man has seen or can see. To Him be honor and eternal dominion! Amen. 1 Timothy 6:13-16*

Mike: The aging process itself should bring us closer to God because it reminds us that our bodies are decaying. That's the hydraulic effect in a nutshell. Each ache and pain pesters us with thoughts of our mortality. Sickness ramps up those thoughts even more. I'm reminded of an old fellow I saw on television. I think he was 107. He said that he was glad to be alive, but he had no friends. They were all dead. "What am I supposed to do?" he asked. "My hearing is shot. So is my eyesight. All I can do is just sit every day." He said that his whole life had changed in different stages and that each stage had made him aware of something different. He didn't make a spiritual reference, but I think that the aging process itself had changed his whole outlook. For a Christian who views life through the microscope of God's Word, those changes involve benefiting from everything God allows us to experience. God opens and closes doors both in aging and in a progressive illness. Those changes have drawn me closer to God and made me more aware of His control.

Tom: I wouldn't want to be that 107 year old guy who can hardly see or hear. It would be hard to study God's Word and witnessing would be limited at best. Even as I say that, I know I am being an idiot. As long as I'm alive, God can use me. I can be a prayer warrior on my deathbed and impact many eternally without anyone even knowing it.

Mike: But God will know and be pleased.

Tom: God is so gracious that even while I am in this lousy body, I can continue growing spiritually and be used powerfully by Him. I need to keep that thought at the forefront of my mind, or I'll begin questioning God's plan for me and others.

Mike: If you are middle-aged and not sick and get up every day and praise the Lord for another day and live in fellowship and do all you're supposed to do, most people don't remark on it. When you are sick and do the same things, for some reason, people interpret that as being out of the ordinary. You are sick—how can you be happy? As if happiness is the monopoly of the healthy and successful!

Tom: My illness seems to have helped others draw closer to God, especially my family. Ten-year-old Katie told Nance the other day that she used to fear having someone she loved die, but since she's seen how happy I am, she has stopped worrying and is happy, too. She knows that being in heaven with God is wonderful, and she's happy for me. But, she concluded, she sure will miss me. Hearing that warmed my heart. While I like knowing she'll miss me, I'm overjoyed that she understands she doesn't need to fear death, that death is only a short separation, not the end.

Mike: Once an illness is known, some friends and family—like Katie—have been motivated to tell us things they've wanted to tell us for a long time and ask us things they've put off asking. It's sure a whole lot easier to speak about God and His plan with someone who has observed our silent witness than to try to do it if our lives stink of worry, anxiety, or discontent!

Tom: A contented lifestyle in the midst of suffering can stimulate a discussion about Jesus with unbelievers. I like that! With some believers, death opens the door to discuss a specific biblical Truth. With others, we are sort of left hanging in the breeze because their spiritual understanding is so shallow they can't fathom enjoying happiness in suffering or being thankful for an incurable illness. And they aren't interested in understanding! They seem to get a perverse enjoyment from their self-induced misery. I even had one tell me, straight-faced, that happiness was impossible for them. They don't worship the same God I do, that's for sure! My patience is sure tested by unhappy believers!

Mike: The world has become so callous to death and suffering that some people are unaffected by anything. Killing an unborn child is less traumatic than losing a pet!

Tom: Or having an appliance malfunction! The other day I wrote a note to the guy who sold me my little John Deere tractor. The first day I talked with him—he's a talkative guy and likes to know his customers—somehow he started talking about a real painful testicle he had.

Mike: Go to a doctor!

Tom: He's a stubborn guy like you, Mike! Along the way, he mentioned that he really likes living. Even though his wife left him two or three years ago, he loves his two daughters and likes doing things with them. He's not ready to die. I told him it's good to enjoy living, but he should also look forward to dying. Life after death is going to be so much better. When he delivered the tractor, I gave him some books by my pastor along with a note thanking him for his good service and encouraging him to read the books and study his Bible. I ended by saying I looked forward to seeing him in heaven. The only way we can truly help others is by giving them the wisdom of God's Word. Anything else we say is like putting a Band-Aid on a ruptured artery! Won't help in the long run!

Mike: First, we have to find out if a person is a believer. What do you think about Jesus Christ? If he has not believed that Jesus died on the cross for him, then the Gospel is the way to go. I haven't been a very effective witness because I haven't done what I just said. I'm trying to train myself so that the next time I talk to someone, I will take full spiritual advantage of the opportunity.

Tom: I'm not as open about God and His Word as I should be either, but it's getting easier. I had a situation yesterday. At an estate sale, I purchased a mini barn to use for my tractor. I met with the man who made it to ask him to add a door. His store had biblical references on the walls, and he gave me a calendar with verses, obviously a Christian atmosphere. We talked easily about Christ, and during the conversation, I revealed that I was in the end stage of cancer. He told several stories of friends of his who had died peacefully and equated their peace to their personal relationship with Jesus as their Savior. I worked the Gospel and biblical Truths into the conversation, emphasizing that joy, peace, and contentment come only to those who know God and His Word. We have to be prepared to turn every conversation to God – to *give an account of the confidence that is in us*[58]— but in a way tailored to that individual and his circumstances. Dying makes my words have more impact. That makes talking to others more exciting for me now.

Mike: Believers who are just starting to learn God's Word can get a series of lessons on basic doctrines and listen to those CDs or DVDs sitting in a comfortable chair at home. And they can rewind sections they don't understand.

Tom: Nancy and I use that handy feature often! Anyone can go to PleromaBibleChurch.org to order lessons and books free of charge.

Mike: Or to AlbanyBibleChurch.org.

Tom: The Holy Spirit is faithful to honor the dedication of those who spend time in His Word. Eventually, all the Truth they've absorbed will start coming together and making brilliant sense. I love it when some piece I've agonized over, trying to understand it—sometimes for years!—suddenly falls into place in my mind. I feel like shouting for joy. Another Hallelujah Moment!

Mike: I enjoy seeing the Greek and Hebrew words used in the original manuscripts of Scripture because often they clarify a principle that is fuzzy in our less precise English language. But I'm sure thankful that I don't have to know the original languages[59] for the Holy Spirit to make the Bible clear to me. I thank God for faithful pastors who

---

58 1Peter 3:15

59 Hebrew, Greek, and a little Aramaic

honor God by learning the languages He chose to use to convey His message to us.

Tom: I find it fascinating—and personally damning—that when our country was founded, many ten year old children could read the Bible in the original Hebrew and Greek! Their parents wanted them to know God's Word in the way God intended when He inspired it. We've lost that thirst for exact biblical Truth, and our country is crumbling from the inside out because of it.

Mike: Another reason to witness boldly. No telling how soon Christianity will be outlawed even here in the Land of the Free. We're headed that way because too few Christians understand God's truth about welfare, economics, crime, government, power—and dying. God covers every issue of life in His Word, including politics. We just have to do the hard work of finding the applicable information, and then we have to let the Holy Spirit guide us in applying it to our thinking and actions.

Tom: Not only do American Christians today—even most pastors!—not know the original languages God designed for His Word, but they don't even know what it says in the English! Can you imagine anyone trusting his brain, which is mortal, to a surgeon who doesn't know anatomy? Yet, believers all the time trust their immortal souls to a pastor who doesn't care enough about God to study His Word in the languages God chose for it! No wonder our freedom is about gone! No wonder Christians are afraid of dying and have such a poor witness in the world! We say we love God, but we sure don't want to have to work to know and obey Him.

Mike: Every moment of our lives should witness to God's never-ending lovingkindness and grace. Maybe the message of our book will encourage some Christians to open God's Word, enjoy it, and share it with others. They'll die happy!

Shout joyfully to the LORD, all the earth. Serve the LORD with gladness. Come before Him with joyful singing. Know that the LORD Himself is God. It is He who has made us and not we ourselves. We are His people and the sheep of His pasture. Enter His gates with thanksgiving and His courts with praise. Give thanks to Him. Bless His name. For the LORD is good. His lovingkindness [faithful love] *is everlasting and His faithfulness to all generations.* Psalm 100

Chapter 9

Sorry, But Since We Live in Satan's World, Pain and Suffering Aren't Optional.

Handling Pain and Suffering with Joy

Consider it all joy, my brethren, when you encounter various trials, knowing that the testing of your faith produces endurance. And let endurance have its perfect result so that you may be perfect [spiritually mature] *and complete, lacking in nothing.* James 1:2-4

Mike: Now to talk about that big bugaboo, suffering. Why do we suffer, and how can we handle the monster that pain and nausea can become?

Tom: Why do people—even wonderful Christians—suffer? Because God doesn't love them? *May it never be,* as Paul would say. NO! NO! NO! as I would say. People suffer because the first man Adam decided to disobey God and thereby brought a curse on all his descendants. Remember that fruit? When Adam sinned, pain and death began plaguing all mankind (and the rest of creation). Every human being is Adam's genetic descendant, whether we want to believe it or not.

Mike: Interesting point! Truth is truth no matter our opinion of it. God is truth so His Word is our only source of truth.

Tom: Death and suffering are abnormal, not part of God's plan for us.[60] Adam's decision to sin brought both death and suffering crashing down on us. Don't curse God for your suffering! If you just can't hold it in, curse Adam! He was the first of us to decide that he didn't need God, that he could do just fine on his own, thank you. What a mistake!

Mike: Adversity is inevitable for all of us. This is Satan's world after all, and Satan can't cause anything worthwhile. Sin is always bad and brings bad consequences —whether we know it is a sin or not. That's one reason we need to study the Bible, so we can recognize sin and say **NO!** to its temptations.

Tom: Looking back, I thank the Lord for things that I used to perceive as handicaps, as suffering. Like my academic lowliness. Nancy knows. She sat with me in the library in college as I struggled to get my B's and C's. I've always understood that if I didn't have the mental capacity to easily understand calculus and physics, I sure couldn't understand the words of the Almighty Creator on my own! I'm just not that smart. I am intensely grateful for God the Holy Spirit's teaching ministry. He helps me understand divine truths I couldn't begin to understand on my own. I also had a profound stuttering speech problem from childhood through college that made me benefit from keeping my mouth shut and not proving how stupid I was! James' exhortation to be quick to hear and slow to speak was easier for me than it would have been without my stuttering. To paraphrase Paul, in my weakness, I become strong because I am forced to trust God exclusively.[61]

---

60 I recommend Clay Ward's booklet *The Abnormality of Death,* available at www.PleromaBibleChurch.org.

61 *Concerning this I implored the Lord three times that it might leave me. And He has said to me, "My grace is sufficient for you, for power is perfected in weakness." Most gladly, therefore, I will rather boast about my weaknesses so that the*

Mike: I've certainly had my share of adversity, and it's been a good thing. Adversity builds strength and reliance on the Creator. The more adversity we have, the stronger we become spiritually— if we use our biblical knowledge during our struggles to have joy and peace even as we suffer. People say that I act as if nothing is wrong even though my body is rapidly failing. Well, nothing is wrong. I'm in God's plan as much now as I was when I was healthy.

Tom: Pain is a progression, and for us pain is progressing like the proverbial speeding bullet. But so what! Suffering comes to everyone at some time! When I'm in pain, I first try to figure out how to get rid of it. Then, I try to consider it all joy[62] because it comes from my loving Father. Again, *my loving* Father.

Mike: My continual prayer even in the midst of pain is that God's will be done.[63] When I think about what I'm going through, I equate it with Scriptural accounts of believers' suffering. How many times have we read the historical account of Samson having his eyes gouged out and not given it much thought? That would have been pretty painful, I'd say, with terrific ramifications and a bit of recuperative time! If Samson could go through that suffering and still turn to the Lord one more time, then I can surely go through this pain without complaining!

Tom: Pain is a gift from God, a grace gift. I know that sounds coun-ter-intuitive, but it truly is. God knows what is best for us. I remember that Truth when I'm wracked with pain. It doesn't make the pain go away, but I remember that God is giving it to me for a purpose and He

---

power of Christ may dwell in me. Therefore, I am well content with weaknesses, with insults, with distresses, with persecutions, with difficulties for Christ's sake; for when I am weak, then I am strong. 2Corinthians 8-10

62 *Consider it all joy, my brethren, when you encounter various trials...* James 1:2

63 *No temptation has overtaken you but such as is common to man, and God is faithful, who will not allow you to be tempted beyond what you are able but with the temptation will provide the way of escape also so that you will be able to endure it.* 1Corinthians 10:13

will never put me in a position that I can't handle with joy.

Mike: I urge myself to suck it up, big guy, and move on! Focus on the Creator, not on the pain! I think of those in Scripture who suffered and the martyrs in the early church—and Christians in anti-God areas today. They are suffering much more than I am, and so are their families. How dare I moan about poor me!

Tom: God has a purpose for everything in our lives, even pain.[64] We grow spiritually when we handle our pain by trusting Him to guide us through it. I don't know the purpose for my pain—I can't know, but I can trust God. I can relax and accept every part of my illness with gratitude and joy.[65] Prayer helps me relax and persevere and keeps me from self-centeredness and self-pity. Prayer is giving thanks for God's gracious character and perfect plan and asking for the strength to endure this suffering and the wisdom to apply His thinking, His joy, to it.

Mike: Doctors ask me if my pain is a number 1 to 10. A blow torch to the armpit might be number 10, and few people experience that kind of fierce pain for long! That thought keeps my pain in perspective. I imagine that I'll reach the blow torch stage eventually, but by then I will have learned to handle lesser pain by trusting God, so I'll be prepared.

Tom: I learned from an oncology tech that if you say your pain is a seven or higher, you have to talk to a nurse. I've never said higher than six so they'll let me go home sooner.

---

64 *For you have been called for this purpose since Christ also suffered for you, leaving you an example for you to follow in His steps, WHO COMMITTED NO SIN, NOR WAS ANY DECEIT FOUND IN HIS MOUTH; and while being reviled, He did not revile in return; while suffering, He uttered no threats but kept entrusting Himself to Him who judges righteously; and He Himself bore our sins in His body on the cross so that we might die to sin and live to righteousness for by His wounds you were healed. For you were continually straying like sheep, but now you have returned to the Shepherd and Guardian of your souls.* 1 Peter 2:21-25

65 *Although He [Jesus] was a Son, He learned obedience from the things which He suffered.* Hebrews 5:8

Mike: I've never told them over six either, but this excruciating pain since my last visit with you will change that. During these new episodes, I keep reminding myself that God is allowing the pain for my eternal benefit. He has also made a way for me to get through it. Pain is totally different from dying. Pain makes itself known—really well known! I have absolutely no question that I am in pain right now, but I have many questions about eternity. You and I know where we're going—to heaven because God promises eternity with Him to everyone who believes in His Son. We know we'll be face to face with the Lord. And we know our pain will be gone! That helps make this pain tolerable. It *will* end! And that end will be glorious beyond my imagination!

Tom: Pain is hugely relative. So far, I haven't had enough pain for it to be an issue my narcotic medications can't mask. I may quit an activity sooner because of pain, but thankfully it hasn't put me in bed yet.

Mike: I hadn't had any debilitating pain either until last week. Hurting so bad I didn't think I could stand it another minute is different from just needing to find a more comfortable position.

Tom: You and I have learned to *endure* and *manage* pain, Mike. About a year ago, a tree fell into the street around the corner so I took my chainsaw over there and went to work. Man, the pain afterwards! That's when I gave the saw to son Tommy. However, I love cutting my own firewood so I figured out how to use the saw without slinging it around, and I stopped lugging the logs. Pain changed my style, but it didn't stop me from doing what I enjoy. In fact, I'm going to get my saw back and cut up some logs this week. *Slowly.* For short periods over several days, maybe a week! And I'm slowly learning to manage the pain. I won't always be able to cut firewood, but God will always make a way for me to endure the pain. I used to emphasize to my surgery patients that they needed to take their pain meds on time so they wouldn't have to play pain catch-up.

Mike: I use a pill holder and have a cheat sheet in the bathroom that lists every pill and the time I should take it. My mind gets so foggy sometimes that I need help remembering.

Tom: I had to buy a new, bigger pill box recently to accommodate my new pills. I'm following my own advice, even getting up at midnight to take pain pills. If I didn't, I might not be able to get out of bed in the morning! We might eventually be unconscious because of our pain meds, but we aren't going to die of pain.

Mike: I have frequently said a prayer that I would be able to stay cognizant for as long as possible.

Tom: That's why I'm hesitant to increase my pain medicine dosage quickly or switch to something that clouds my mind even more. Eventually, I may run out of options, and the only recourse will be knocking me out with drugs. Even as I say that I think of Nancy's dad who was 92 when he died of thyroid cancer. He hadn't been able to eat much for several months or drink at all near the end. He was in pain, but he didn't take many medications. He was still getting up, dressing, and doing light chores the day before he died. And he was privileged to die at home. Nancy and her siblings appreciated having him alert at the end, writing notes and mouthing words because the tumor kept him from speaking. Her mom died of breast cancer and was the same way until the last days. They both loved the Lord and trusted him. I hope I can tolerate the pain, too, so I can enjoy my last days, and my loved ones can enjoy being with me. But the Lord's will be done.

Mike: That's the problem with medications, finding the balance between mitigation of pain and becoming incognizant.

Tom: And that is achievable as long as we allow God to help us withstand the pain that can't be eradicated without putting us in a coma.

With Him, all things are possible.[66] On our own, pain is unbearable, nasty, the ruler of our thoughts and lives.

Mike: I've seen too many people die before the cancer killed them, the drugs taking their minds from them.

Tom: My mom was unconscious for quite a while before she died. That's a crummy way for loved ones to say goodbye. Right now I'm not bed-ridden, just nap-ridden! Usually, you can find me lying on the couch, resting or reading. My reading is restful because it focuses me on my Creator. I was lying in bed at 4 this morning enjoying listening to the rain, and I decided the best way to describe my body is as a burden, a dead weight. I feel weighed down by it.

Mike: I often wonder how I'm going to have enough energy to lug it around for another day.

Tom: But we won't be our bodies' prisoners for long! Knowing I'll soon be with my Lord and Savior and have a new but perfect body puts a little spring back into my step—as long as I don't take many steps!

Mike: Or spring too high! It's interesting how fast things change. Surprises are the constant in this stage of dying.

Tom: Those dramatic changes help us remember that everything is in the Lord's hands. No matter how well we have prepared to face dying and death, we still have to continue learning and depending on Him because we have no idea what surprises tomorrow may bring.[67]

---

66 *I know how to get along with humble means, and I also know how to live in prosperity; in any and every circumstance I have learned the secret of being filled and going hungry, both of having abundance and suffering need. I can do all things through Him who strengthens me.* Philippians 4:12-13

67 *Trust in the LORD with all your heart, and do not lean on your own understanding.*

Mike: I've always drawn a little word picture in my mind of the fact that from the moment we are born, our bodies are going downhill. Our bodies are decaying. We might say that the dying process starts at birth, more slowly for some than others!

Tom: Obviously, death is a bigger deal than, say, quitting my profession. Then, I had to make changes that would affect my staff, patients, and family, but I had more control over those changes, and I could have reversed them later if I had wanted. Death is final and irreversible. We are leaving our loved ones, at least for a short while. However, if they accept God's will for our lives and theirs, any depression or self-pity they have can be reversed. They can learn to be thankful for God's timing for our deaths and to rejoice in our homecoming to heaven.

Mike: It is fruitless to react to death any differently than to any other of God's tests. If I had an accident and was paralyzed, I'd have to apply many of the same biblical principles I am now applying to dying. The challenge to someone who is paralyzed, blind, or without limbs is the same as ours. Will we wake up the next day with smiles on our faces, or will we blame God or someone else? God expects us all to apply His Word to every trial in life, including dying. He wants us to trust Him and relax.

Tom: We can't think that it would be easier to be paralyzed than to be facing death. The Lord makes that choice. He knows our innermost thoughts and needs. He knows exactly what will most benefit us eternally.

Mike: Death is the finality in dealing with Satan's world and takes on more significance than anything else in life. I look at death as another phase in life but with more significance.

In all your ways acknowledge Him, and He will make your paths straight. Do not be wise in your own eyes. Fear the Lord and turn away from evil. It will be healing to your body and refreshment to your bones. Proverbs 3:5-8

Tom: Sometimes, God allows suffering to discipline us so we will recognize our sins, confess them to God the Father, and come back to Him—again, God-given suffering for our benefit. To me, God's discipline is a private, personal thing. No one can look at another person and know why he is suffering—though it may seem obvious if his lifestyle is conspicuously immoral! I know some suffering in my life came from God's discipline. I don't need to discuss that with anyone but the one I sinned against and God. As David wrote after his evil against Uriah and Bathsheba, *Against You* [God], *You only, I have sinned and done what is evil in Your sight so that You are justified when You speak and blameless when You judge.* Psalm 51:4

Mike: I definitely went through a good deal of suffering for discipline when I was out of fellowship for those ten years. That suffering finally drove me back to church, back to God. I knew I was messing up. God made it very clear. I think it would have been as ridiculous for me to say "Why me?" when I was suffering discipline as for a six year old to ask his father, "Why me?" when he is about to be disciplined. We have no more right to question our loving Creator than a child has to question his loving father.[68] We all benefit from fair discipline.

Tom: But the child still does question his punishment! And so do we if we judge our punishment or suffering through our shortsighted arrogance—if we go the "why me" route—rather than remembering God's omniscient love of us.

---

68   *It is for discipline that you endure. God deals with you as with sons for what son is there whom his father does not discipline? But if you are without discipline, of which all have become partakers, then you are illegitimate children and not sons* [haven't believed in Christ as Savior]. *Furthermore, we had earthly fathers to discipline us, and we respected them. Shall we not much rather be subject to the Father of spirits and live? For they disciplined us for a short time as seemed best to them, but He disciplines us for our good so that we may share His holiness. All discipline for the moment seems not to be joyful but sorrowful; yet to those who have been trained by it, afterwards it yields the peaceful fruit of righteousness.* Hebrews 12:7-11

Mike: I try to never question or second guess God's plan for my life. I want to deal with each adversity biblically and move on. When they were quite young, two of my grandsons, Jacob and Austin, were in a horrible accident that took their father's life and almost theirs. Their truck was on fire. The boys were strapped in, and their seat belts were tight because of the accident. The situation seemed hopeless, but God had placed three good Samaritans right behind them when they crashed. Those three struggled to loosen the boys' seat belts. One of them had a fire extinguisher in his camper and ran back to get it. The other man and a lady kept working in the midst of the flames and finally got Jacob loose. She carried him to a safe place and continued caring for him until medical help arrived. The two men finally got Austin loose—his leg was wrapped around the floor gear shifter. I'm telling this story because those Samaritans—and they were good, indeed—never asked, "Why me?" They just jumped into the fiery vehicle and did what needed to be done. While they didn't want recognition, one of them worked for the city and was told he had to get recognized to improve the city's image. The other guy refused to allow anyone to write anything that glorified his effort. After the lady knew the baby was okay, she simply disappeared. To this day, we don't know who she was. Those people handled the crisis in the way we should handle every part of pain and suffering in our lives; do what is right and move on. When the doctor says you're dying of cancer, you should say okay and continue to leave your life in God's hands.

Tom: I feel sorry for believers who think their illness is part of suffering for Christ. Worldly suffering, the same suffering that even unbelievers go through, is different from suffering for Christ. Our illness, the destruction of our mortal bodies, certainly isn't unusual, and it equally certainly isn't suffering for Christ. The Apostles and martyred believers in past generations suffered because they stood firm in Christ as the only Savior. Many believers have been tortured, stoned, hung upside down on a cross like Peter just because they refused to stop proclaiming Jesus Christ as Lord and Savior.[69]

---

69   *After calling the apostles in, they flogged them and ordered them not to speak in the name of Jesus and then released them. So they went on their way from the*

Dying Happy

Mike: I think of Christians around the world today who suffer atrocities because they refuse to bow the knee to Islam, the main Baal or Moloch of today. Christians in America have few opportunities to suffer for Christ. We can go out and set up a tent and teach Christ risen, and no one will stone us or burn our houses or our church. We won't be persecuted.

Tom: For us, suffering for Christ is limited to subtle discrimination, maybe gossiping about us because we walk in a way different from the world. The time seems to be fast approaching when we will suffer as have other believers because of our stand for Christ, but our suffering now is limited to the problems of living in a fallen world with death an inevitable component of it.

Mike: We can't be certain of God's reason for our suffering, but we know it's for our good and His glory. My family had a graphic illustration of God's grace in our suffering! One day, when Patsy was alone with her two babies, Jennifer and Cindy, and pregnant with Lori, eighteen-month old Cindy spied a glass of tea and climbed up on the kitchen table to get it. She picked it up but dropped it on the floor, and it broke with the bottom on the floor and jagged pieces of glass sticking up. She looked over at it and fell headlong off the table and right into the glass. It sliced both sides of her face. It literally fileted both her cheeks. Everyone was distressed, wondering why God had let this tragedy happen to this beautiful child who always had a smile on her face. After the accident, Patsy was holding Cindy and happened to be under a bright lamp. She noticed that something white covered one of Cindy's eyes. The next day, she took Cindy to the local optometrist, who examined her and said he didn't see anything wrong. Before the accident, Cindy had been having seizures that even adult medications couldn't control so, thankfully, Patsy doubted the optometrist and still suspected something truly was wrong. She called Cindy's neurologist, who told her to bring Cindy to him immediately. Patsy drove two

presence of the Council, _rejoicing that they had been considered worthy to suffer shame for His name._ And every day, in the temple and from house to house, they kept right on teaching and preaching Jesus as the Christ. Acts 5:40-42

hours that Saturday afternoon to reach a clinic that should have been closed. Instead, the neurologist had contacted twenty-three specialists—twenty-three! That wouldn't happen today for sure, not with socialized medicine! They all came to his office and examined her that afternoon. The pediatric ophthalmologist said that he was almost certain she had retinoblastoma, but he'd have to run tests to be sure. Patsy took her back to him on Monday, and Cindy had eye surgery on Wednesday. That fall saved her life because it jarred the tumor loose from the back of her eyeball. The tumor then migrated to cover her eye. Cindy never had another seizure! I can remember her at church with her head covered with bandages, a patch covering her empty eye socket, and a smile lighting her face. She was just as happy as before.

Tom: What a great example of the blessing of suffering!

Mike: After Patsy and I were married, we went to a seminar about nutrition in Atlanta. The speaker, who was in his late eighties, was founder of the Atlanta Eye Clinic. After his speech, we told him that our child had survived retinoblastoma. He started weeping and said he had never known of anyone who had survived that dreadful disease. Since then, diagnostic procedures have advanced so they can discover the tumor before it is fatal; however, God used a horrendous fall to diagnose it for Cindy. Without the trauma of the fall, she would have died.

Tom: Did the scars and lack of an eye affect her badly?

Mike: No, she's never let it bother her. In her teens, she was a little self-conscious, wondering if people noticed her glass eye, but she didn't obsess about it even then. She's much stronger because of it. Now, as a nurse, she's more empathetic with her patients. She is one tough cookie. When she lost her husband in the accident, she was better prepared to face it because she had seen God's kindness in her earlier adversity.[70]

---

70 *Therefore humble yourselves under the mighty hand of God so that He may exalt you at the proper time, casting all your anxiety on Him because He cares for*

She handled his death much better than most would.

Tom: I'm guilty of not always remembering that God's love will turn everything into good if I trust Him.

Mike: We should never doubt His love for us, that's for sure. One of my favorite parts in the New Testament is about the pot. I'm talking about a pot the potter made, a pot with an attitude.[71] What's the pot going to do—call the potter out because he doesn't like the way he made him? That particular passage has always fascinated me because so many Christians live their lives questioning God the Potter's plan for them. I live with the knowledge that I am the pot, God made me, and I don't have the right to complain about my design or usage. I'm just looking forward to whatever He continues to pour out on me.

Tom: Sure, we can reach a high level of spiritual understanding without having a severe illness, but God says we all have to be tested and retested often to insure we really understand and use all we've learned of His Word. Will I get upset when the toilet floods all over the floor? If a raccoon gnaws its way into my house—and I have one of those bandits working on it right now by a dormer window in our house! What about if I am treated unfairly? Passed over for a promotion? That's not going to happen to me, but it could happen to a friend. Will I tell him how unfair it is or to be thankful because God has

---

you. Be of sober spirit. Be on the alert. Your adversary, the devil, prowls around like a roaring lion, seeking someone to devour. But resist him, firm in your faith, knowing that the same experiences of suffering are being accomplished by your brethren who are in the world. After you have suffered for a little while, the God of all grace, who called you to His eternal glory in Christ, will Himself perfect, confirm, strengthen and establish you. To Him be dominion forever and ever. Amen. 1Peter 5:6-11

71 *On the contrary, who are you, O man, who answers back to God? The thing molded will not say to the molder, "Why did you make me like this," will it? Or does not the potter have a right over the clay, to make from the same lump one vessel for honorable use and another for common use? Romans 9:20-21*

plans for him in his present position? What about if I break a leg, something that could easily happen with this type of cancer? If I'm happy and content during all such minor sufferings, then I'm prepared to have joy, peace, and contentment in the granddaddy of all tests, my own death or that of a loved one.

Mike: And God will continue blessing us! Because Jesus Christ satisfied God the Father's righteousness and justice on the cross, He is free to use His love to go crazy blessing us. To paraphrase God's Words in Malachi, "I will open for you the windows of heaven and pour out for you a blessing until it overflows."[72] You and I, Tom, are experiencing a remarkable over-flow of blessings in this, our final stage of life on this earth.

Tom: Just as we have been inundated with blessings throughout our lives! God is good. What an understatement!

Mike: Dying is the final test that all the lesser sufferings have pre-pared us to pass with peace and joy. If I choose to depend on God completely during the less difficult tests, I'll breeze through the final one victoriously. I rejoice that you and I, Tom, have reached that final test and are about to go home!

Tom: Like savoring dessert after a long and satisfying meal!

Whom have I in heaven but You? And besides You, I desire nothing on earth. My flesh and my heart may fail, but God is the strength of my heart and my portion forever. For, behold, those who are far from You will perish; You have destroyed all those who are unfaithful to You. But as for me, the nearness of God is my good. I have made the Lord God MY REFUGE SO THAT I MAY TELL OF ALL YOUR WORKS. Psalm 73:25-28

---

72 Malachi 3:10

Chapter 10

Set Your Biological Clock on God's Time!
Waiting with Patience

There is an appointed time for everything, and there is a time for every event under heaven—a time to give birth and a time to die. Ecclesiastes 3:1-2

Mike: I used think it would be neat to know the day I was going to die, but I've lost that desire. When I fulfill my responsibilities and learn and obey God's Word, I'm doing exactly what I would do if I knew.

Tom: We may not dwell on how much time we have left, but you and I, Mike, are at the end of our game. We're in overtime with only one time out left! Maybe! Without divine intervention, we both will die soon. I have tried to prepare—to tie up—everything from finances to the maintenance of the house and yard so that Nancy will have the easiest possible time after I'm gone. You've seen the stacks of firewood in our backyard. She can have fires in our wood burning stove for at least the next two winters. I try not to put off doing anything I'm still able to do since I don't know when my time—and energy!—will run out.

Mike: A practical approach demands that we take care of our affairs. Having a will written by a competent attorney has to be at the top of the list. No procrastination there for my wife's sake! What a headache for her if I put that off until too late!

Tom: E. M. Bounds wrote the perfect answer to why we don't need to worry about the timing of our dying. "God's man, living in the center of God's will, is immortal until God is through with him." We are immortal as long as God wants us to be! I love that! When we die, we merely move into permanent immortality. This cancer has finally started me enjoying each day, not wasting it trying to make tomorrow special. I should have been doing that all along, appreciating each day's blessings, enjoying my immortality.

Mike: If we spend our time crossing off the days, we lose the joy of living our lives to the very end. We short-change ourselves. God gives us each day just the way it is for us to enjoy. Each day brings just what we need, so why ruin it by worrying about tomorrow?[73]

Tom: Why not revel in our immortality?!

Mike: In my opinion, the more we dwell on how long a doctor has given us, the more likely we are to meet his goal! I like to say to people that I'm not going to die one minute before or one minute after the perfect time the Lord has chosen for me to die. Why should I give the timing of my death any consideration? It's in His hands. I sure have no power over it. In the end, neither does any doctor.

Tom: Nancy's dad was a lung disease specialist. He said that often those patients he thought were sure to get better died, and those he thought couldn't survive did. He gave them the best care modern medicine could provide, but life and death have always been God's responsibility. God confounds the wisdom of men, reminding us of His power and brilliance and our lack of both. No man, even the best-

---

73 *"So do not worry about tomorrow for tomorrow will care for itself. Each day has enough trouble of its own."* Matthew 6:34

educated doctor, has any control over God's plan. I appreciate my doctor's openness with me in relating his life-expectancy experiences with patients with a similar cancer, but he isn't omniscient. He can't possibly know exactly when or how I will die. Doctors just don't know much.

Mike: Takes one to know one! We may as well relax, get out of God's way, and let Him take care of everything. He sure doesn't need our help or ideas. My job is to make myself available to His service each day I wake up, not to tell Him what to do.

Tom: You and I have already proven that no one can predict how much time we have. I was told three to five years. Seventeen years later, my body is wasting away, but I'm still enjoying life.

Mike: The hardest part for me is thinking about my family because not all of them are facing my death with big smiles on their faces. Thankfully, our wives trust the Lord as we do, but some of those we love haven't made it their habit to know and trust God. I'm concerned for them, wishing I could change them. But I can't. The most difficult day I've ever had was when I had to tell Patsy my cancer was back. I hated seeing my smiling, vivacious wife realize she wasn't going to see me live with her much longer. Seeing her shock was tough, really tough. Now, we rejoice in every moment we have together.

Tom: I used to be almost disappointed when I saw the doctor and learned that my disease had not progressed much. I was so ready to finish my race and be with God in heaven! Knowing that this is terminal brings the temptation to want it to speed up. I've learned to resist that thought and be thankful for each day. I want to be here as long as I can for Nance and those I love as well as for those who depend on me. Every minute I can hold a grandchild is precious to me! However, when I get the news that my cancer is continuing to progress rapidly, I don't feel sad because I'm prepared for the inevitable and thankful for the present. I'm thankful that my future in heaven is secure, too.

Mike: My oncologist said that the progression of my disease has been exactly as he expected with one exception. It has progressed more slowly than he is accustomed to. He has no explanation but is thankful. He said his pet name for me is Turtle. I told him that the turtle still crosses the finish line.

Tom: Yes, Mike, you *will* finish the race! You will die. So will I. And the Lord knows the perfect time for both of us. If I live moment by moment in His will, if I don't dwell on the past or worry about the future, I am living exactly as He commands. Living one day at a time, enjoying and utilizing it to the maximum, makes both living and dying so much easier. I have no reason to question or doubt God's timing because He gave me today with all its blessings. His mercies never cease.[74]

Mike: It's selfish on my part, but I'd like to see my grandsons graduate from high school. That's not going to happen. The Lord knew that in eternity past, long before He created the world. He has always known everything, even exactly what would have happened if we had made different choices along the way! And for every person in the world! For sure, He is not going to make a mistake about the time of my death! We have to work with the time God gives us, and we are given only one day at a time.

Tom: After my diagnosis, my mom worried about my dying, having to witness her child's death. She couldn't understand why Nancy and I weren't upset, too. Then, though she'd always been healthy and led a vigorous life, she died long before I will. We can't presume to know God's exact plan for our lives or our deaths. We must live each day as if it is our last and not worry that it might be. We can't know God's timing, but we can know that it is perfect.

---

74 *The* LORD'S LOVINGKINDNESSES [loyal love] *indeed never cease for His compassions never fail. They are new every morning. Great is Your faithfulness.* Lamentations 3:22-23

Mike: That's like my mother, who is eighty-one years old. She keeps saying that children aren't supposed to die before their parents. I tell her that's not written anywhere in the Bible. She insists that it doesn't matter if it's written or not because it's just not supposed to happen! This illness has forced me to take inventory of myself and accelerate some of my plans. I hadn't expected to sell my business nearly this early in my life. That wasn't my timing, but it has allowed me to spend the resulting extra time in the Word. That's a big deal! For me, a really big deal! How God sold my business for me is a neat story. I hadn't advertised it for sale or even put a sign in the window, but one day, a man walked in off the street and offered to buy it pretty much right then and at a good price. I couldn't believe it! God took care of that problem before I had done more than consider it! What grace! Especially in this bad economy!

Tom: God does the seemingly impossible with ease, doesn't He? I'm guilty of not giving Him that opportunity often enough. Like you, I'm thankful that the Lord has given me this extra time to prepare, actually to *catch up* in my spiritual life. If I'd died suddenly, I wouldn't have felt this urgency to know God better and to appreciate all my blessings, especially my family. I don't think I ever could have known this incomparable joy and peace without this cancer. That in itself is enough reason for me to be thankful for my death sentence.

Mike: A child could walk outside and have a meteor fall on him. We just don't know when God will take us home.

Tom: So we'd better tell our grandchildren about Jesus Christ as Savior early and often. Even they have no guaranteed life expectancy.

Mike: Their warranty could run out at any moment!

Tom: We say our days are numbered now, but God has always known that number. We just like to think they won't come to an end—at least not this soon. It's amazing how much younger sixty-eight is now that I've reached it!

Mike: I used to think over-the-hill was forty! The ignorance of youth!

Tom: Recently, a friend asked me how I felt about death. My answer? Bring it on! I look forward to being with my Savior. My biggest dread about the process of dying is being dependent, having to consume someone else's time and life just taking care of me. I shouldn't dread that because even in that condition, the Lord can use me. Taking care of us sacrificially while we are dying may be the best way—maybe the only way—for those we love to reach the mental state of dependence on God that is necessary for true happiness in this life. It may force someone to get into a routine that glorifies God more than he would have without it.

Mike: We don't want to get to heaven and find out that the *only* reason God left us on earth was as a test for others! We want to be His shining light, not the curmudgeon who is nothing but a pain to everyone!

Tom: We can be a blessing to some and a test for others, I suppose. Not everyone likes being around a happy dying man! My cancer was diagnosed as extremely aggressive so I have hoped that when we ran out of ways to slow it down, death would come quickly. Pure selfishness! God knows what's best for me and those I love so I need to praise Him for each day He gives me and be thankful for my final days, whatever they hold for me, no matter how long the suffering lasts.

Mike: I've had lots of people ask me why God has given me this extra time. The only possible answer is that He's not finished with me yet. I have work left to do in His plan. I am comforted knowing that when my time to die comes, I'll leave my sorry body on earth, but my soul and spirit will go to heaven.

Tom: In fact, angels will carry your soul and spirit, the real you, into the very presence of God![75]

Mike: That's an exhilarating image, isn't it! Every bit of God's Word that I have learned and used will go with me and be a blessing to me there, too. That means that the most important thing I can do with my remaining time is fill my soul with God's Word by being totally available to Him until I check out. Even though I'm dying, I want to be as eager to serve God as the prophet Isaiah. *Then I* [Isaiah] *heard the voice of the Lord, saying, "Whom shall I send, and who will go for Us?" Then I* [Isaiah] *said, "Here am I. Send me!"*[76]

Tom: "I'm here waiting eagerly for You to use me, Lord! I'm ready, willing and able—but only if You guide me in doing the work. I'll mess up if I try to do it on my own."

Mike: That's it—being available to His service and trusting Him to lead us in doing it right. I've been going to treatment for so long that most of the patients with whom I started have died. I'm still here. We can't question God's decisions. We can't ask why we got extra days and they didn't. Or why this guy was run over by a bus and never got to tell his wife goodbye. Or why my grandsons lost their daddy. We could ask so many questions, but we shouldn't ask them because only God knows the reasons, and He does everything with our best interests in mind. Questioning God only makes us miserable.

Tom: It sure doesn't help! God's timing for pain as well as for death is perfect. He doesn't let anything happen to those who obey Him until they are ready spiritually to handle it with joy and peace. We can trust Him to shelter us under His wing throughout every adversity.[77]

---

75 Luke 16:22

76 Isaiah 6:8

77 *He who dwells in the shelter of the Most High will abide in the shadow of the*

Mike: God takes care of all our family and friends as well as us. He weaves everything together. What is happening to us with this cancer is part of that timing.

Tom: Thankfully, it's His timing and not ours! He does everything perfectly. We sure don't!

And when the living creatures give glory and honor and thanks to Him who sits on the throne, to Him who lives forever and ever, the twenty-four elders will fall down before Him who sits on the throne, and will worship Him who lives forever and ever, and will cast their crowns before the throne, saying, "Worthy are You, our Lord and our God, to receive glory and honor and power for You created all things, and because of Your will they existed and were created." Revelation 4:9-11

Almighty. I will say to the Lord*, "*My refuge and my fortress, my God, in whom I trust!*" For it is He who delivers you from the snare of the trapper and from the deadly pestilence. He will cover you with His pinions, and under His wings, you may seek refuge. His faithfulness is a shield and bulwark.* Psalm 91:1-4

Chapter 11

To Beg or Not to Beg: That Is Not the Question
The Power of Persistent Prayer

Therefore I say to you, all things for which you pray and ask believe that you have received them, and they will be granted you. Whenever you stand praying, forgive if you have anything against anyone so that your Father who is in heaven will also forgive you your transgressions. Mark 11:24-25

Tom: Prayer is our great weapon in this life and never more so than as we pound on death's door. God commands that we ask, seek, and knock.[78] We speak and God answers.

Mike: My first prayer every morning is thanksgiving to the Father for another day of life. I'm thankful for every day God gives me because it is another day for me to fulfill His plan for my life, to be a positive influence on someone or a witness to someone. My goal is to be available for whatever He wants me to do.

Tom: My waking prayer is thanks for bringing me another day closer to eternity. I ask God for the strength to endure, the wisdom to make

---

78 *"Ask, and it will be given to you; seek, and you will find; knock, and it will be opened to you. For everyone who asks receives, and he who seeks finds, and to him who knocks it will be opened."* Matthew 7:7-8

good decisions, and the humility to spend as much time as possible in fellowship by realizing when I sin. God has removed most distractions from my life so my sins aren't as obvious to me now. I'm not sinless perfection—you don't need to nod your agreement so vigorously, Mike! I know I have sinful areas in my life, especially in my thinking, sins that I'm oblivious to. Thankfully, God understands my sin blindness. When I commit those unknown sins, I invariably sin in a really obvious way. 1John 1:9 is one of my go-to verses. In it, God promises that when I tell God the Father the sins that I know are sins, He cleanses me from *all* unrighteousness, too, meaning all my unknown sins.[79]

Mike: God is wonderful to us, isn't He? He never neglects to provide everything we need to serve Him, including an easy way to get back with Him after we sin. Just one more example of His amazing grace.

Tom: He wants us to recognize our sins so He gives us plenty of examples of different types of sin, especially in the Old Testament. David was a sinner of rare ability, a murderer, rapist, adulterer, deceiver, and polygamist to name a few. A Sinners' Hall of Fame top vote getter for sure! Yet, God called David a man after His own heart. How could perfect God say that about such a despicable sinner? Because the moment David recognized his sins, he consistently and humbly confessed them to God. And God immediately forgave him!

Mike: God knows we are going to sin. That is never in question. What we do about it isn't nearly so certain. Will we humble ourselves before Him in acknowledgement of them, or will we pretend what we did wasn't really so bad? Will we harden our hearts to God and our sins? Or will we come back to Him?

Tom: That's why King Saul, David's predecessor as king, was a huge failure in God's eyes. He was a moral man and proud of it. He hung

---

79 *If we confess our sins, He is faithful and righteous to forgive us our sins and to cleanse us from all unrighteousness.* 1John 1:9

onto his sins, never humbling himself by admitting them to God.

Mike: Since I have stopped going to my sign and print shop and facing all the challenges and temptations with customers and employees, it's easier for me to keep from sinning. I question myself constantly because I've never stayed in fellowship with God this long! What is going on here?!

Tom: I know what you mean, Mike. No frightened patients, no employees with problems, not as many temptations to be impatient or frustrated! After we confess our sins, we can get on with our prayers. When God answers those prayers, our lives change.[80] So do the lives of others we pray for. I wonder how many times my neglect of prayer kept me and those I love in bad situations and bad habits for longer than necessary. God promises He'll answer *all* prayers that agree with His Word.[81] I want to emblazon that on my mind so I can unleash that unlimited divine power for myself and others. The one thing I've never prayed for is to be cured of this cancer. I honestly believe it's my time to go home. I'm ready whenever God is ready to take me.

Mike: I feel that way, too. I'd enjoy having more time with my family, but they will spend eternity with me in heaven so a few minutes more on earth isn't a pressing issue.

Tom: Keeping my mind on eternity puts the seeming problems on earth into perspective. They are like a grain of sand in a sea of diamonds, not worth fretting about! In his book on prayer, David Jeremiah wrote that the great prayer warrior Andrew Murray (1828-1917) said, "Having so much to do one day, I had to add an extra hour of prayer." Add an extra hour of prayer!? How often do I pray for even one hour? I am ashamed at the poverty of my prayer life. David Jeremiah suggests

80 *The effective prayer of a righteous man can accomplish much.* James 5:16b

81 *If you abide in Me, and My words abide in you, ask whatever you wish, and it will be done for you.* John 15:7

praying with an empty chair in front of you so you can picture yourself having an intimate conversation with your Father.

Mike: An interesting idea because when we pray, we mentally enter into our Father's heavenly throne room. What pressure that puts on me to pray with reverence and humility, to remember that I am praying to my Father, the great God who created everything!

Tom: I'd better approach Him with fear and trembling plus immense gratitude that He cares so much for a nothing like me!

Mike: When I pray for myself, I pray that I'll use God's Word in my soul to be delivered *through* the cancer, to glorify God *through* it. I like it when someone learns that I am seriously sick and smiles and says, "Praise the Lord. He's going to use you." I've felt better the few times that happened because that person understands that God allowed this cancer for my good. God will benefit me in important ways He couldn't have if I had remained healthy.

Tom: We both want the Lord to use us as witnesses to influence people by the peace in our souls even as this cancer ravishes our bodies. That's our prayer.

Mike: In prayer, I constantly use the word challenge, that God the Father will challenge me to remain in fellowship by not sinning and challenge me to apply His Word to my decisions and actions. If I can just stay in fellowship—confess to God the Father each sin as soon as I commit it— and then make my life line up with the commands in His Word, I'll be okay. I'll automatically please Him.

Tom: Until you choose to sin again, of course! We both know how easy that is. And God the Holy Spirit won't *force* any of us to acknowledge our sins or to apply God's thinking to our decisions. We have to make those choices ourselves. But He uses circumstances and people and all sorts of things to influence us to choose to get back into His will. This cancer is a good example of the power of a circumstance to improve our God-focus.

Mike: If I'm praying for someone and don't know for sure that he is saved, I pray that he will be challenged with the Gospel so that a decision for Christ might be evoked. For a struggling Christian, I pray that he will be challenged with God's Word so that a decision to study it seriously might be evoked.

Tom: Challenged. That's a great way to say it. You're asking God to put the *unbeliever* into a situation that will force him to make a choice. Will he choose Christ or reject Him again? And you are asking God to force the *believer* to see that he must make a choice. Will he choose to immerse himself in God's Word, or will he continue immersing himself in himself? Will he trust God or won't he? Will he be content or defiant and miserable?

Mike: I heard a pastor the other day say that when you pray that way you're giving the person you're praying about a chance to vote. We get to vote often each day, each time we consider whether we will follow God's plan or sin, whether we'll be happy or not, afraid or content. I think most believers have the wrong idea when they pray for cancer patients. All they think about is getting us out of our "tragic" situation. How can we get this poor guy cured of this cancer? My prayer isn't to get out of my situation but to glorify God as long as I am in it. I want to fulfill God's purpose for this cancer. I know you feel the same way.

Tom: I do. When I pray for someone who is sick, I'm drawn to pray that if it's the Lord's will, let him have his illness removed. Regardless, I pray he will be able to apply whatever Bible knowledge is in his soul to his problems so he can have peace, joy, and contentment no matter what happens.

Mike: I've had people express astonishment that I haven't asked the Lord to take this cancer away. I don't see the need. It's brought me much greater blessings than good health ever did. Why would I want that to end?

Tom: I'm the same way. But I do follow God's command to ask Him for wisdom in dealing with my disease and its unpleasant consequences.

Mike: And He says you've got all you need between those black covers of your Bible!

Tom: True, but God *commands* me to ask for wisdom to live my life according to His will.[82] He won't give me that wisdom, the only wisdom there is, out of empty air. If I haven't consistently and intensively studied the Bible, the Holy Spirit cannot remind me of verses and biblical principles that will give me wisdom to endure my problems with joy and peace.

Mike: The Bible gives a precedent for praying for self and others who are sick. After Paul lost his healing power, which God gave to him solely to verify that Paul's words were divinely inspired, he prayed for his sick friends to be healed. He believed in God's power to heal. He knew absolutely that God does as He promises. But he also knew that God is the only One who knows what is best for each one of us.

Tom: I appreciate having others pray for me. When my pain is suddenly worse, I wonder if one of my prayer warrior friends has been

---

82 *But if any of you lacks wisdom, let him ask of God, who gives to all generously and without reproach, and it will be given to him. But he must ask in faith without any doubting, for the one who doubts is like the surf of the sea, driven and tossed by the wind. For that man ought not to expect that he will receive anything from the Lord, being a double-minded man, unstable in all his ways.*
James 1:5-8

distracted from his praying. Without question, the people who help me the most are believers like Daniel, those who have enough spiritual understanding to pray effectively, constantly, and importunely. That's one of E. M. Bounds favorite words for prayer, and I'm adopting it. We are to constantly bring our requests before God until He answers them in His timing. Then, we can stop that prayer. But continue others!

Mike: My universal prayer for someone who is sick is 1. That the Lord will meet his needs. 2. That He will bestow mercy on him. And 3. That His will will be done.

Tom: What else can we say? God has promised He will supply all our needs, and what we need is strength and guidance to enjoy every moment of His plan for us, even the dying part.

Mike: Believers struck with an illness should avoid hustling around begging people to pray for them. We don't need a bunch of people who don't even know us praying for us, but a few who are praying effectively make a world of difference.

Tom: I appreciate those who are praying that I will have the strength to endure and that my needs will be met, that I will apply God's Word appropriately. I want them to pray that way for Nancy, too, and for the rest of my family. We need that invisible support from others. When I get an email or note from someone who unexpectedly took the time to encourage me, I know they are thinking about me and praying for me. The same is true of those who give me books and goodies they think I might enjoy. I can't begin to express my pleasure in their kindness. And, of course, I love visits. Don't we all feel better around those who shine with love for us?

Mike: We could say a prayer for us is an *invisible* visit that shines with love! Sometimes, I'm just sure someone is praying for me right then because I feel so much better all of a sudden. I was at my barber's several months ago, and he realized I must be starting a new treatment. Remember the strange and noticeable changes that accompany each new treatment? He noticed. No one else was in the shop, and when I got ready to leave, he asked if he could pray for me. He took my hand and said, "Dear heavenly Father, please meet this man's needs and may Your will be done. In the name of the Lord Jesus Christ, Amen."

Tom: And you said a resounding Amen.

Mike: I did, indeed. That was one of the most squared away prayers I've heard yet. I hope he has kept praying on my behalf!

Devote yourselves to prayer, keeping alert in it with an attitude of thanksgiving. Colossians 4:2

Chapter 12

What on Earth Do I Say to Someone Who Is Dying?

Finding the Right Words

Pleasant words are a honeycomb, sweet to the soul and healing to the bones.
Proverbs 16:24

Tom: Some people just don't know what to say to us now. They are uncomfortable because they don't understand that death is a beginning, not the end. Death is separation, not annihilation. They feel sorry for us when they should be congratulating us. We're about to be promoted home!

Mike: A few years ago, I was going through one of my worst chemotherapies. I'm beginning my eighth one now. I looked really rough and felt even rougher. My voice was raspy. A lady came into my shop, and my disease made its way into our discussion. She said she felt so sorry for me. I said, "I want to ask you something. Do you think either one of us is going to get out of this alive." She said, "No." So I asked her, "Do you know if I am going to die before you?" She said, "No, I don't." I said, "Then, we're both rowing in the same boat because we're both going to die, and we don't know who's going first." That conversation reminded me of how much in charge God is. He decides who has the next number. Far be it from me to question omniscient God! Some guy told me recently, "No one wants to die, and no one wants anyone else to die." If God honored that wish, we'd be so old we couldn't even bend over to pick up something to eat!

Tom: When people say, I feel so sorry for you, they are walking around in denial, not wanting to face the reality that everyone is in the process of dying—though I will admit that you and I are speeding more rapidly than most toward total decay. That lady who said she felt sorry for you probably meant she was sorry you were at a time in your life when you are actively facing death. She may have been afraid to get to that point herself.

Mike: Makes me sad for her because she can't avoid death. We would all benefit if we lived our lives as if death were staring us in the face that very day.[83] Our priorities would sure change. At least, I hope they would.

Tom: Sports, TV, computers, games, hobbies all sap time from our lives. They may be okay in very limited quantity, but how many of us, especially in America, aren't victims of our own overindulgence? Having limited energy has helped me curb my own excesses—another benefit of this cancer.

Mike: I wonder if most people aren't fixated on keeping busy because they don't want to hear the eternity that God placed in our hearts at birth.[84] They don't want to have to turn their lives over to Him. Have

---

83 *So teach us to number our days so that we may present to You a heart of wisdom.* Psalm 90:12

84 *He* [God] *has made everything appropriate in its time. He has also set eternity in their heart, yet so that man will not find out the work which God has done from the beginning even to the end. I know that there is nothing better for them than to rejoice and to do good in one's lifetime; moreover, that every man who eats and drinks sees good in all his labor—it is the gift of God. I know that everything God does will remain forever; there is nothing to add to it and there is nothing to take from it, for God has so worked that men should fear Him.*

you noticed how almost everyone these days has a phone glued to his ear? Doesn't matter if a live human being is sitting across from him! People can't even drive without wanting to be distracted! They sure aren't interested in considering life after death!

Tom: A friend sent me an email recently, saying she hadn't communicated with me earlier because thinking about me made her sad. I wrote her back, saying, "It's making me sad to think that I'm making you sad."

Mike: I think people appreciate having us take the edge off our situation with humor, even feeble attempts. They relax when they find we are willing to laugh at our problems and to talk calmly about our own deaths, a subject that frightens most participants.

Tom: One concern I've had recently is that I may be a little too matter of fact about dying. Just the other day I was talking to a neighbor I hadn't seen in a long time. He's let me cut firewood on his property in the past and, pointing to a dying tree, said, "You need some exercise, don't you?" I said, "I really don't need exercise right now. I'm in the latter stages of this prostate cancer." He said he was sorry to hear it. I told him about the cancer in the context of other things and didn't mention it again. Later, he said, "You referred to your cancer lightly. I'm sorry to hear about it." Others have mentioned that I don't seem concerned about my cancer. I'm not, but is there some negative aspect to sounding too casual?

Mike: Taking dying for granted seems logical to me, but I, too, have been surprised to find that even most believers view death as complicated and undesirable. They think relying on God and forgetting about the problem like we try to do isn't taking it seriously enough. And thanking God for cancer? They'd say that's pure lunacy! Sad for them.

Tom: Nobody can do anything to stop the course of my disease, but

Ecclesiastes 3:11-14

that doesn't make me sad. I *am* sad when a believer shows he has no understanding of God's kindness in allowing suffering into my life. I wish everyone could understand the high level of joy and peace my cancer has made possible and that they could experience it, too.[85] This is the highpoint of my life.

Mike: Most people aren't around dying people who take their dying well, so they are wary about saying anything. It's a real bummer when someone starts crying and carrying on and acting like a nut, but that does happen. Then, I've had to deal with those who declare I shouldn't accept this disease. I made the mistake of mentioning my cancer to one of those. He jumped all over me, saying I accepted the cancer when I said it was mine. I must never do that. Pure hogwash! How could this cancer be anyone else's? Our faith is tested by other people, even believers; that's for sure.

Tom: That poor guy just revealed that he is a stranger to God and reality.

Mike: Only a few people have reacted like that, but they sure made me uncomfortable.

Tom: Most people react with a mild level of sadness. "If I can do anything for you, just give me a call."

Mike: "My grass needs cutting. Can you be here by eight?!"

Tom: That goes back to bearing one another's burdens. The other day, I was talking with Clay about spiritual gifts in the local church, and he

---

85 *But let all who take refuge in You be glad. Let them ever sing for joy and may You shelter them so that those who love Your name may exult in You for it is You who blesses the righteous man, O LORD. YOU SURROUND HIM WITH FAVOR AS WITH A SHIELD.* Psalm 5:11-12

explained that as pastor, he avoids seeing a need and then delegating it to a church member. Instead, he follows the biblical example and waits for someone to recognize the need and volunteer to take care of it. The same should be true as we bear the burdens of our fellow saints. We should work to recognize their needs and then take care of it rather than waiting to be asked. We need to be doers of the Word[86] and think of others as more important than ourselves. Recently, I was too weak to finish splitting some firewood in my backyard even with a hydraulic splitter. Tommy and Clay recognized my need, and instead of spending that Saturday splitting their own wood, they came over and split and stacked mine. I really appreciated their thoughtfulness. I find it hard to ask people to do things for me. That's probably wrong on my part. Maybe they don't volunteer because they don't think they can meet my expectations.

Mike: To heck with our expectations! We just need help. When I realize someone truly wants to help, I call him when I need something, and, so far, everyone has been pleased to help. They make it easy to ask.

Tom: The generosity of others is a source of such joy to me. The greatest compliment anyone can give me is to speak to me just as they always have, not like I'm a freak or fragile because I'm face to face with dying.

Mike: You're right, buddy. We just want to enjoy a level of normality. We're the same old cotton pickers we always were even though our bodies are going downhill fast!

Bear one another's burdens and thereby fulfill the law of Christ. For if anyone thinks he is something when he is nothing, he deceives himself. But each one must examine his own work, and then he will have reason for boasting in regard to himself alone and not in regard to another. For each one will bear his own load. Galatians 6:2-5

---

86 *But prove yourselves doers of the word and not merely hearers who delude themselves.* James 1:22

Mike and Jennifer

Chapter 13

You Mean I Can't Just Die? I Have Preparations to Make?

Decisions to Make about the Physical

Do nothing from selfishness or empty conceit, but with humility of mind regard one another as more important than yourselves. Do not merely look out for your own personal interests but also for the interests of others. Philippians 2:3-4

Tom: So far we've concentrated on the spiritual, but dying also brings a steady supply of odd decisions to make. How will we spend those last months? And what about the funeral? Let's discuss some of those so others won't have to face them alone for the first time like we did.

Mike: I have it in my mind that I want to die in my own home. I want people coming to see me to be comfortable. I'm so crazy I already have it planned where everyone will sit while we visit.

Tom: Sounds like you've given it a lot of thought.

Mike: I have. A friend on the brink of death asked me to visit her, but no one had made any arrangements. I ended up kneeling on the floor. She couldn't really see me, and my knees aren't as young as they used to be. I'm getting our bedroom ready now so that Patsy won't have that extra burden when I'm bedridden.

Tom: But you aren't going to demand that people visit you. Your friends and relatives know that. I can't think of anyone in my family who will think they have to be with me, holding my hand. Don't get me wrong—I'll enjoy any and all visits. I'm enjoying having more visits now. For me, if the dying becomes so ugly or complicated that Nancy doesn't have the necessary skills, I want to go to a hospital or a nursing home. I was interested to learn that feeding isn't even necessary at the end. People can go days, even weeks, without food or drink before they die, and they don't suffer because of it. Nancy's stepmother didn't eat or drink for several weeks. The nursing home nurses told Nancy that many relatives want to do something, anything, and demand that their dying loved ones be fed and hydrated through tubes. In truth, the nurses said, filling their bodies with nutrition they can't assimilate makes the physical process of dying more unpleasant for them.

Mike: God knows what is best for each of us, and it may include going without food or water for a while at the end. I'm blessed because Cindy has plenty of vacation time built up and wants to be with me for as long as necessary as I face the end of this dying process.

Tom: She'll be able to anticipate your needs much better than a staff nurse could. And you'll want to be with her as much as possible anyway.

Mike: When I was in chemotherapy, I told Patsy that I bet most of the nurses had either gone through cancer themselves or with a loved one because of their level of empathy. Later, a nurse told me that all but three of the nurses had requested to be in the cancer clinic because of personal experiences with cancer. I said, "I can name those three." I knew who they were because, though they did their jobs well, the same level of compassion just wasn't there.

Tom: They were doing their jobs without understanding the underlying needs of dying patients. That's similar to the way Christians stumble through life when they haven't taken time to know God through studying His Word. They want to do right, but they've never learned what God expects of them so they fail. I agree that being at home during the dying phase is the way to go if possible. I'm keeping my options open since I don't know what my physical condition will be at the end.

Mike: Speaking of the end, a man in our church, crazy but a nice nut, underwent hemorrhoid surgery and was in the hospital for longer than he thought necessary. He told his wife he was going to get on his knees so she could assess what they had done down there. She was down there inspecting when his doctor walked in the door. He took a quick look, said, "Since I'm no longer needed…" and walked out.

Tom: What a hoot! Sure proves the point that hospitals and privacy don't go together.

Mike: I hope I have humor to the end,[87] and I hope it's never crude.

Tom: What kind of final arrangements are you making for yourself, Mike?

Mike: Yesterday, I went to a tailor to have a pair of trousers altered. I'm losing an abundant amount of weight these days even though I make myself eat. The mortician was there. I told him that it looked like I was going to need his services sooner rather than later. All the jokes we've shared in the past were looking at later rather than sooner, but the tables are turned. He asked me how much longer I thought I had. I told him six months was probably the earliest. Among other things, he

---

87 *"If you do well, will not your countenance be lifted up? And if you do not do well, sin is crouching at the door, and its desire is for you, but you must master it."* Genesis 4:7

recommended I go to the funeral home's web site and fill out a form. That would save time at my first conference with him.

Tom: We've already met with a funeral director. He gave us one of those forms to fill out before we return to make further arrangements. We went to see him early because we were in the process of having some farm property zoned for a cemetery. He owns cemeteries so we knew he could give us good advice. He explained that vaults to hold the casket, whether concrete or metal, aren't mandatory under law, but many cemeteries require them because they keep the ground from sinking. Makes mowing easier.

Mike: My vault's going to be concrete.

Tom: That's what we were thinking since it will probably be less expensive than metal. I was pleased that our property was later approved for burial sites. I've enjoyed hunting quail and dove there for years and feel it is the right resting place for me. Nancy and the kids will like having me at rest in the midst of God's creation. My appreciation for His work has increased since my illness because I observe nature more closely now and appreciate more intensely His creative powers. I don't merely enjoy being in it, away from the pressures of the world, as I used to. One of my first jobs when we moved to the smaller house we're living in now was to build a bird feeding station outside our kitchen window. I love teaching the grandkids about the bright goldfinches and tilt-tailed wrens, cardinals that come in pairs and black-capped chickadees, blue jay bullies and timid titmice.[88] Each child is eager to be the first to spy a woodpecker. Will it be a downy or a hairy or maybe a red-bellied? Crows come with their raucous caws, and the kids shoo them away. We marvel at God's grace in giving us such variety in His creation. We thank Him for not filling the skies with crows only! What

---

88 *Are not five sparrows sold for two cents? Yet not one of them is forgotten before God. Indeed, the very hairs of your head are all numbered. Do not fear. You are more valuable than many sparrows.* Luke 12:6-7

a privilege to share my love of God's creation with those I love! I don't take that opportunity for granted as in the past.

Mike: So you may be the first rentee at your cemetery?

Tom: An older gentleman at church is vying with me to see who will be first, but it looks like I'll beat him. Our church is planning to build on five acres at the same site so the cemetery will be part of our church's property. I've talked to the neighbors, and they have no problem having a cemetery there. In fact, their college age daughter has terminal cancer so the cemetery may be a source of comfort for them, too. Using my tractor to keep the area mowed until then will be a challenge. I sit on the machine and let it do the work for about 10 minutes. Then, we both rest for about 20. Takes a bit more time than it used to! I'm just thankful I can be out there.

Mike: I'm going to have a service at Albany Bible Church. Then, they'll have a graveside service in Enterprise, Alabama, my hometown. My dad and grandmother are buried there.

Tom: We're planning to have a service for me at the funeral home since our church building is small. Our pastor, who is also a son-in-law, which makes it doubly nice, will officiate. I'd just as soon go quietly, but a funeral is such a good opportunity to give the Gospel to those I care about. They will be face to face with death and may be more ready to accept Jesus Christ's great gift of salvation, to believe in Him as Savior so they can have eternal life with Him forever.

Mike: At the graveside service for my father, the pastor unexpectedly called on me to say the final prayer. I was glad for the opportunity. Then, at the funeral of my great-aunt last week, when the whole family got into the room before we went to sit as a family, my brother, who is a minister and was officiating the funeral, called on me to say a prayer. On those two occasions, the Lord used me to say things those people might not have heard otherwise. I put it to them! Someone told Patsy later that those few words were powerfully packed. I recently went to a funeral where the preacher and I were the only ones who had on ties. And one of the pallbearers actually had on a t-shirt and a pair of shorts! To many people, going to a funeral is no different than having a beer, totally unimportant. They feel no need to show respect for the one who died or the One who gave him life. There's an emptiness in many people today, the worldly people this materialistic culture has produced.[89]

Tom: That spiritual emptiness is the tragedy of our age. Makes leaving here easier. Do you already have a headstone?

Mike: It's a perpetual care cemetery so all we'll have is a bronze plaque. Easier maintenance for them.

Tom: We'll probably decide on a dual tombstone for both Nancy and me when we make our final visit to the funeral home. We'd like to have some verse on it but haven't decided which one for sure. But I just read this epitaph and may have to reconsider: "Here lies the body of Solomon Peas, under the grass and under the trees; but Peas is not here, only the pod. Peas shelled out and went to God!"[90] I just love that! Rhyming Northcott might not be so clever! Have you talked about a casket?

---

89 *But because of your stubbornness and unrepentant heart, you are storing up wrath for yourself in the day of wrath and revelation of the righteous judgment of God, who will render to each person according to his deeds: to those who by perseverance in doing good seek for glory and honor and immortality, eternal life; but to those who are selfishly ambitious and do not obey the truth but obey unrighteousness, wrath and indignation. There will be tribulation and distress for every soul of man who does evil, of the Jew first and also of the Greek, but glory and honor and peace to everyone who does good, to the Jew first and also to the Greek. For there is no partiality with God. Romans 2:5-11*

90 Mark Hitchcock, <u>55 Answers to Questions about Life after Death</u>

Mike: I'm going to have a wooden casket.

Tom: We've already chosen the least expensive metal one. I sure don't care what my dead body lies in!

Mike: I'm not interested in spending a lot of money on my box either. On any of the arrangements for that matter.

Tom: What do you think about an open casket?

Mike: Doesn't bother me a bit.

Tom: Does me. Nothing looks more dead than a body without a soul and spirit. I'm not going to have any type of viewing.

Mike: I understand that, but I'll probably have an open casket. It's been my family's tradition, and it is an object lesson for youngsters. I've found it an opportunity to tell my grandkids that the body isn't the real person. It is just the tent we live in until we go home to be with the Lord where we belong. I've found that those who have seen dead animals and dead people seem to handle death better than those who haven't.

Tom: That's one reason I take some of my grandchildren with me whenever I hunt quail and dove. They help clean the dead birds so Nancy can cook them. Bacon-wrapped dove is at the top of our "great food" list. I'm not going to have an open casket because I'd like my family's last memory of me to be a live one.

Mike: Even if I take my grandson Peyton's suggestion and am buried in my Hawaiian shirt, Bermuda shorts, and cap, what does it matter? I won't care, and I want my family to be as comfortable as possible in a difficult situation. I'm not going to rise up saying, "That's not what I wanted!"

Tom: That might cause more of a stir than the Hawaiian shirt!

Mike: Be fun, wouldn't it! My father's father died before I was born, and my grandmother remarried. I was six years old on that Easter Sunday morning when my Dad got the phone call from his mother, telling him that his stepdad had died in his sleep. I went with dad to the other side of town to visit her. My granddaddy was lying in the bed dead. He looked the same but really weird. I didn't understand at the time, but the soul and spirit give the body its character, personality, and aliveness.

Tom: That's why I'm not going to have an open casket. That brings us to the subject of cremation versus burial.

Mike: I'm not sure it makes a difference.

Tom: I felt the same way until recently when I started studying it more. Now, I wonder if burial isn't more in keeping with God's Word. All the patriarchs from Abraham on down were buried. Jesus, the Son of God, Son of Man, was buried in a tomb. The clincher for me is that *God Himself* buried Moses. Even baptism relates to being buried in Christ and resurrected to life.

Mike: And pagan cultures *do* tend to gravitate toward cremation. You are about to convince me.

Tom: If I'm telling people that I'm going to heaven rather than to the Lake of Fire, why do I want burning my body to be my last choice on earth? I want both my life and death to be the best testimony they can be, and burial seems to send a message more in keeping with my beliefs. I don't want to even hint that fire might be part of my eternal future because it sure isn't! When Christ judges my life, yes, but fire after that, no. Heaven illumined by God's light is the only place for me.

Mike: Some believers are cremated whether they like it or not. The soldier who is hit in the middle of his chest by a big ordinance and vaporized. Or someone who dies in a flaming car or plane.

Tom: God knows where every atom of every believer's body is! He'll have no trouble resurrecting every little piece into a perfect resurrection body.

Mike: Another example of His faithfulness to us. For a long time, I wanted to be cremated. After my dad died, I decided I wanted a conventional funeral, including burial. I guess those points you made must have been floating around in my head without my realizing it.

Tom: Even though we need to make arrangements for our dead bodies, we'd better keep our focus on our eternal souls. That's the key word: eternal. We should be concentrating on filling them with morsels from God's Word whenever we have a free moment.

Mike: And then putting everything we learn into action, being a light in a dark and dying world. Whatever the details of our final arrangements, we want God glorified, the Gospel given, and the pressure on our loved ones minimized.

Jesus said: *"You are the light of the world. A city set on a hill cannot be hidden; nor does anyone light a lamp and put it under a basket but on the lampstand, and it gives light to all who are in the house. Let your light shine before men in such a way that they may see your good works and glorify your Father who is in heaven."* Matthew 5:14-16

Chapter 14

An End that Is the Beginning? Impossible!

Entering Permanent Eternal Life

The wife of Christian theologian Francis Schaeffer wrote at his death: *It was 4 am precisely that a soft, last breath was taken and he was absent. That absence was so sharp and precise. Absent. As for his presence with the Lord I had to turn to my Bible to know that. I only know that a person is present with the Lord because the Bible tells us so. The inerrant Bible became more important to me than ever before. My husband fought for Truth and fought for the Truth of the inspiration of the Bible —the inerrancy of the Bible—all the days that I knew him…through my 52 years of knowing him. But—never have I been more impressed with the wonder of having a trustworthy message from God, an unshakeable word from God—than right then! I feel very sorry for the people who have to be "hoping without any assurance"…because they don't know what portion of the Bible is myth and what portion might possibly be trusted.* Louis Gifford Parkhurst, Jr., Francis Schaeffer, the Man and His Message, 1985.

Mike: My father's business partner died in his sleep one night. He was an older man but hadn't been sick. The next day, we were downtown in our little city at the hardware store, drinking a Coca Cola. You remember those old red metal Coca Cola machines with glass bottles? Joe, the man who ran the store, had been sick for about ten years. He had a colostomy back when colostomies were no fun. My brother asked him, "Did you hear that Herman died last night?" He hadn't.

"Herman just went to sleep and didn't wake up." And Joe said, "That's a great way to go." Then, in a second, he added, "And cheap, too." For years, Joe had suffered numerous health problems and rising bills, and his friend had just gone to sleep and not awakened!

Tom: Herman didn't suffer any pain, but he didn't have the privilege of preparing for death either. We say Herman didn't wake up, but he did.[91] And he was in heaven! Now that's a great wake-up call! The Lord often describes death as going to sleep in Him, probably to help us welcome death. The last few minutes before we go to sleep each night are peaceful. We are relaxed and comfortable. That's the way we should be as we face our last days on earth.

Mike: I've been with several believers when they died, and they always had a peaceful end.

Tom: Interesting that the Bible never refers to an *un*believer's death as going to sleep. I can't imagine the horror of those who don't see heaven but the fiery furnace yawning before them, ready to roast them forever. They must be in an agony of fear at that moment. One second they are on familiar earth and the next in agonizing hopelessness and pain. I thank God that Christ died for me and took the eternal punishment of sin from me so that I can be sure I don't have eternal fire in my future!

Mike: When we go to sleep, we also wake up. Another comforting

---

91   *But we do not want you to be uninformed, brethren, about those who are asleep so that you will not grieve as do the rest [unbelievers] who have no hope. For if we believe that Jesus died and rose again, even so God will bring with Him those who have fallen asleep in Jesus.* 1 Thessalonians 4:13-14

thought.[92] For a child of God, dying won't be agonizing in those last minutes but comfortable and reassuring, thanks to the Lord's plan. He loves us. That coupled with His assurance that we will be face to face with Him immediately after death shouldn't provoke anything but peace and gratitude.[93]

Tom: Speaking of the joy of going to sleep, we also rejoice when we've tossed and turned in pain and are finally able to go to sleep at night. We wake up in the same fallen world with the same ailments, but at least we had a short vacation from it as we slept!

Mike: One of the drugs they give me has the side effect of keeping me awake. The night of that treatment I lie there wide awake, not able to do anything about it. Sleep is good!

Tom: God wants us to face death—whether our own or others'—with absolute confidence and peace. He gives that ability to those who have been faithful in learning and obeying His commands. What a treasure for the Father to give His children!

---

92 *Blessed be the God and Father of our Lord Jesus Christ, the Father of mercies and God of all comfort, who comforts us in all our affliction so that we will be able to comfort those who are in any affliction with the comfort with which we ourselves are comforted by God. For just as the sufferings of Christ are ours in abundance, so also our comfort is abundant through Christ. But if we are afflicted, it is for your comfort and salvation; or if we are comforted, it is for your comfort, which is effective in the patient enduring of the same sufferings which we also suffer; and our hope for you is firmly grounded, knowing that as you are sharers of our sufferings, so also you are sharers of our comfort. 2Corinthians 1:3-7*

93 *For I am already being poured out as a drink offering, and the time of my departure has come. I have fought the good fight. I have finished the course. I have kept the faith. In the future, there is laid up for me the crown of righteousness, which the Lord, the righteous Judge, will award to me on that day and not only to me but also to all who have loved His appearing. 2Timothy 4:6-8*

Mike: Christ promised that He would prepare a place for us so I know every moment in heaven will be absolutely wonderful, beyond my most flamboyant desires. My last breath will take me to one incredible home!

Tom: I don't need to be hoping that the end of this suffering will come quickly because every breath I take is important in giving me time to prepare for eternity—and more time to enjoy this escalating peace, joy and contentment I have now! I shouldn't wish this or that anyway! Wishes are based on emotion, not God's Word. So are what if's. What if I'd seen the doctor sooner? What if I'd taken more medications or more treatments or different ones? What if I'd not let my son go on that trip so he wouldn't have been killed? We can what if ourselves into complete misery!

Mike: God is in charge. He never makes mistakes, and He always does what is best for us and everyone else. Our job is to trust Him no matter our situation. He *will* give us what we need. But that's not necessarily what we want.

Tom: That's because we're too stupid and short-sighted to know what is best for us. At least, I am.

Mike: This week, a lady in our church told me, "My husband's death was very ugly." And it was. I told her that the Lord had ordained that death for him because great blessings would come from it, not only for him but for those who love him. That's all anyone can say. Until the end, any adversity we face strengthens us spiritually—if we depend on God and obey His commands through it. Pain and suffering benefit us in eternal ways we are incapable of appreciating.

Tom: Of course, if we scream out "Why me?" it's not our spiritual life that is strengthened but our self-centered arrogance in doubting the goodness of God's plan for us. I've found that, because I'm suffering, God has given me many opportunities to witness to others about His faithfulness and goodness. I am hopeful those opportunities will increase the closer I get to death. I want to show my love for my God even as I take my last breath.

Mike: I tell people, "I hope I die with a big smile on my face." I go into rigor with this great big smile pasted on my face, and the mortician is like, "How do I get this grin off this guy's face?" Wouldn't that be great!

Tom: What a perfect way for you to check out, Mike, since your smile is your trademark! Enoch was another happy guy. The account of his life and death fascinate me.[94] He loved the Lord and walked with Him right into eternity. Ray Stedman wrote, "Enoch became forever the example of what death is to the Christian—only an incident, hardly worth mentioning. That is the reality that Enoch discovered by faith." So easy. We go to sleep and awaken with the One we've been following through life. What a glorious awakening that will be!

And Jesus answered them, saying, "The hour has come for the Son of Man to be glorified. Truly, truly, I say to you, unless a grain of wheat falls into the earth and dies, it remains alone; but if it dies, it bears much fruit. He who loves his life loses it, and he who hates his life in this world will keep it to life eternal. If anyone serves Me, he must follow Me; and where I am, there My servant will be also. If anyone serves Me, the Father will honor him. John 12:23-26

---

94 *Enoch walked with God; and he was not, for God took him.* Genesis 5:24

Mike and Jennifer

Chapter 15

How Can *I* Be Related to *Him*?

Family, Wonderful Family

For this reason, I bow my knees before the Father, from whom every family in heaven and on earth derives its name, that He would grant you according to the riches of His glory to be strengthened with power through His Spirit in the inner man so that Christ may dwell in your hearts through faith and that you, being rooted and grounded in love, may be able to comprehend with all the saints what is the breadth and length and height and depth and to know the love of Christ which surpasses knowledge, that you may be filled up to all the fullness of God. Ephesians 3:14-19

Mike: My family is extremely important to me. I treasure them above everything but my Savior. Every time something new with this cancer happens to me, Patsy and I sit down with our three daughters, our two sons-in-law, and the three boys and have a family meeting. We answer any questions and encourage them with God's faithfulness.

Tom: You're blessed to be able to all meet together often. It's hard to get our children alone together even though everyone lives within walking distance. When the adults in our family are together, no one is left to watch the kids. We have fifteen from barely a year to eleven, Olivia, Katie, Ethan, Sam, Tucker, Andrew, Reagan, Renee, Jonathan, Thomas, Hannah, Emma Claire, Abigail, Evelyn, and Lydia. Great kids! I just had to mention them by name. They are my best medicine. Now that I am nearing the end of my life, my desire is to leave them impressions and thoughts that will help strengthen and influence them to accept God's joy and peace and to serve Him with happy hearts. I want to spend my time creating remembrances that will be positive for their spiritual growth, not doing the silly things I might have done were my leaving them for a while not so real. I want them to know without a hint of doubt that we'll all be together again soon in heaven.

Mike: I think back to when I was a kid and the changes various losses in my family caused. Thinking about the changes that my death will bring heightens my realization that I really am going to die soon. I've thought about recording a video for each of my grandsons that might help them, but I wonder if that is the best thing to do. Patsy will have to help me decide. She and I consciously work to grow spiritually ourselves so that God will bless them through us. I want to do all I can to influence them while I'm still on earth. The boys have reached the age that they may be introspective about my death. Who knows? They may be drawn closer to the Lord because they start thinking more deeply about spiritual truths then. My prayer is that the Lord will use my death to challenge them from His Word.

Tom: My little grandkids will understand that Grampy is in heaven and be glad for me. Those kids pick up on more than we realize. Our everyday attitude of joy is more visible to them, perhaps, than to adults.

Mike: My death will affect Jacob and Austin tremendously. They've spent at least one night a week with us since they were little. They practically lived with us after their daddy was killed. For over a year, I was like a surrogate father to them.

Tom: So you have a special bond with them. Another of God's gracious blessings.

Mike: Special, indeed. All the years our girls were growing up, we never missed a Bible class. There is no merit in that, but we tried to give them a foundation in God's Word by setting an example at home and through church. Patsy and I believe that our greatest gift to our children is to continue growing spiritually. If we remain faithful to God, His grace to us will overflow to them. From the outside looking in, you and Nancy have great, great children. They make a good impression.

Tom: We couldn't have better children, including the four who married our four. We're so thankful they love the Lord and serve Him daily. Like all parents, we see potential problems we'd like to steer them clear of, but some of those lessons they seem to want to learn the hard way.

Mike: You want to save them from hitting their heads against the wall like you did!

Tom: How right you are! Why should they have to suffer like we did if we can prevent it. Experience is a tough teacher. When I was first diagnosed, Tommy, our youngest, was in Marine basic training at Parris Island. He wasn't allowed to receive phone calls so we sent him a letter about my diagnosis and hoped his sergeant would let him have it. We didn't want him to learn about the cancer from someone who wouldn't give him the divine perspective. The sergeant broke protocol and allowed him to call us. What a blessing that was! The other three were away at college and handled it well also. We have been blessed immeasurably by their steadfast trust in their Lord. Nancy and I are so grateful for God's grace to them because we certainly weren't perfect parents. What an understatement!

Mike: Jacob and Austin learned to be open about their dad's death. They are comfortable talking about death. That is different from most families that have never faced death and so have a traumatic experience when death hits.

Tom: Nancy's stepmother died recently, and the grandkids talk about heaven and getting to see her there someday. They're excited about seeing everyone—Moses, Daniel, David, with Jesus at the top of their list. The younger ones shake their heads sadly and say they won't get to see Goliath, though, because he didn't believe in Jesus.[95] They see death as a good thing because they will be with the God who loves them. When Ethan was about three, he decided it would be fun to climb out his second story bedroom window. When our daughter Melissa explained that he might die, he said that was okay because he'd get to go to heaven! Heaven is more real to my grandkids than Australia—or Kentucky for the younger ones!

Mike: Patsy and I married when our youngest, Lori, was only 18 months old. She never saw her natural father enough to really know him. All three girls, Jennifer, Cindy, and Lori, are as much mine as if they were mine genetically, so precious to me. While each of their responses to my impending death is different and I have trouble knowing how they are handling it, I know they love me and understand and accept what is happening.

Tom: I'm thankful that Nancy will be here to comfort the little ones after I'm gone. She's already decided she won't remarry because if God wanted her married, He'd keep me alive.[96] She knows that not remarrying isn't necessarily best for others, but it is for her, especially since God tells older widows to remain unmarried so they can give biblical wisdom to younger women.[97]

---

95 For Goliath, the Seed of the Woman in Genesis 3:15

96 *But I say to the unmarried and to widows that it is good for them if they remain even as I. But if they do not have self-control, let them marry for it is better to marry than to burn with passion. 1Corinthians 7:8-9*

97 *Older women likewise are to be reverent in their behavior, not malicious gossips nor enslaved to much wine, teaching what is good, so that they may encourage the young women to love their husbands, to love their children, to be sensible, pure, workers at home, kind, being subject to their own husbands, so that the*

Mike: We know a lady whose husband died at a relatively young age. She stated that she would never remarry. She is happy with her decision because she was totally healthy in her approach to her husband's death. Some spouses immediately remarry; some never remarry; some go into the depth of depression; some handle it with flying colors. I would hope every Christian would handle the remarriage decision in the way God commands, with confidence, knowing that he/she is doing God's will according to His Word.

Tom: I know people who regret remarrying. They rushed into it, hoping to end their loneliness or recreate the pleasure of their first marriage, but they didn't get what they expected. They may have married the right person, but they didn't wait long enough. A husband and wife are one person according to God.[98] When half of you is wrenched away in death, it takes a lot of time for adequate healing. Whether we are single or married, slave or free, God expects us to be content in our current situation.

Mike: Because Patsy and Nancy have a healthy amount of God's Word in their souls, they have a better understanding of God's will. They'll know the right decision about remarriage and be comfortable about it.

Tom: I'm thankful the Holy Spirit will fill their consciences with disquiet if they are heading the wrong way. As we've said many times, God always takes care of everything. We don't have to be concerned about our wives after we are gone.

Mike: It *is* tough on the spouse who is left behind, really tough. I think Patsy and Nancy probably suffer more than we do even now, watching helplessly as we go through pain. Patsy sits there, hurting

---

word of God will not be dishonored. Titus 2:3-5

98 Genesis 2:24

to see what is going on with me. She doesn't like seeing me go down-hill. She wonders what will happen when I go home to the Lord. She doesn't fear being alone, but she wonders. She will miss me, but she knows we will soon be together again, this time in heaven with our Savior. That is another comfort that brings joy and peace to both of us.

God is our refuge and strength, a very present help in trouble. Therefore we will not fear though the earth should change and though the mountains slip into the heart of the sea, though its waters roar and foam, though the mountains quake at its swelling pride. Psalm 46:1-3

Chapter 16

The Very Real, Undeniable, Awesome Blessings of Incurable Cancer

Now to Him who is able to do far more abundantly beyond all that we ask or think according to the power that works within us, to Him be the glory in the church and in Christ Jesus to all generations forever and ever. Amen.
Ephesians 3:20-21

Tom: At some time in all our lives, I think we all become curious about dying, what it will be like. You and I know the answer. We know that the greatest peace and joy possible in life come during the days of greatest suffering. We are dying, and we rejoice in having reached that high point, that exclamation point in our lives.

Mike: I've been so graced out by this illness. I yearn for others to experience this remarkable, indescribable grace as they head for home with their Lord. Cancer, any fatal illness, exerts a definite pull toward God. Thankfully, since this cancer came on the scene, my tendency to be Christ-centered has grown and flourished. I feel so much closer to my Creator now than before. Why? Facing death helped me realize that life and time were racing to an end for me. The time I have left has become more vivid. I'm more conscious of my Creator, His blessings, the work He is doing in my life and in the lives of those around me, and the fact that Jesus Christ controls history. I could see all those truths before, but knowing that I'm dying has accentuated my God-vision. I would be a pitiful employee right now because my mind is so totally occupied with the Lord. That poor attempt at humor is to show that my focus is firmly on the Lord now.

Tom: For me, too, the greatest blessing of this cancer has been having my attention changed from the distractions of the world to the Lord and His Word. I am motivated to do a better job of prioritizing the way I spend my time because I have been forced to admit that time is running out. It was before, too, but I was too blind to realize the implications and buckle down to the job God placed before me, stuffing my soul with His Word, obeying everything I learned, and trusting Him no matter what.

Mike: Knowing I have limited time has made me question the things I always thought were important. I want to be sure I spend my remaining time exactly as God desires. The caveat is that I cannot know God's desires unless I know His Word, the only place He has given them to me.

Tom: One blessing of every day I remain here is learning to know God better, to appreciate Him more. I want Him to greet me as a dear son when we meet face to face, not as one of the black sheep in His family! My inner peace shows me that God is with me every moment. I can look back and better see His omnipotent and gracious fingerprint on every moment of my life. Certainly, He has visibly piled blessing on blessing during this time with cancer. He has directed every event to bring me to this wonderful conclusion, standing on the edge of eternity, eagerly waiting to see my Savior face to face.[99]

---

99 *I pray that the eyes of your heart may be enlightened, so that you will know what is the hope of His calling, what are the riches of the glory of His inheritance in the saints, and what is the surpassing greatness of His power toward us who believe. These are in accordance with the working of the strength of His*

Mike: The Lord has every event in our lives interwoven for our benefit. We're like Esther, having a definite role in God's plan. How phenomenal is that! We can't begin to comprehend His care of us, every detail handled perfectly for our benefit and His glory.

Tom: In the little time I have left, I want to demonstrate God's love through my life, to gain and maintain control over being judgmental (a weakness for me), to view everyone with grace, not just be nice to them but work hard for their good. I'm going to quote E.M. Bounds again. His book on heaven spoke to me in the way I needed—and at the right time. "Christianity must not only present a model to the world, but it must provide practical illustrations as well…To put others alongside of us is generous and gracious, but to put them before us is divine." I want to put others before me.

Mike: Could we say that, be at this level of spiritual maturity, if we hadn't had this cancer? No, I definitely don't believe we could! Our suffering was necessary to bring us to a closer walk with God. He's looking for invisible heroes, believers who do what they are supposed to do, make themselves available to His service, and let Him use them, knowing all glory belongs to Him. But we have a better plan. We don't want to be invisible because we have lust patterns in our souls that make us want to be known as great Christians. We think ourselves better than we are. We don't want God to use us. We want to use God. That's the crux of the human shortcoming.

Tom: God knows what's best for us, what's best for each individual Christian, not necessarily what seems best to us on earth but what He knows is best for us to gain our rewards and glorify Him eternally. Eternity is forever. Life is just a blip on the radar of eternity, though

---

might which He brought about in Christ, when He raised Him from the dead and seated Him at His right hand in the heavenly places, far above all rule and authority and power and dominion, and every name that is named, not only in this age but also in the one to come. Ephesians 1:18-21

we like to think that what we do here will have major, lasting importance. No one will remember who invented the computer or cell phone any more than we remember who invented the pencil. Kings and presidents? Here today and gone from all memories tomorrow.[100] Earthly awards and recognition are as fleeting as our bodies. Once our immediate family is gone, we'll be nothing more than a face in a snapshot—and that snapshot will turn to dust, too. The only pieces of our lives that have lasting value are those that glorify God both now and forever. God remembers them and will reward us accordingly. No other rewards or awards matter.

Mike: For years, I watched my father suffer from Alzheimer's. He went through many stages because he lived so long. I used to sit in his room with my mother, watching him lie there, knowing nothing. Mother would say how pitiful he was. I'd tell her that God blesses us in everything but that she would probably have to wait until she got to the other side to understand those blessings. Scripture doesn't tell us for sure, but I think that in heaven we will be able to see God's plan in our lives, all the blessings that we didn't appreciate or recognize at the time. We'll be shocked at the immense number certainly but also, I think, by the great ones that came because of our suffering. What an eye-opener that will be, to realize God's continuous care of us, how He lovingly nurtures us every moment of every day!

Tom: The prophet Jeremiah wrote that only God knows the plans He has made for us.[101] God has known His plans for us forever, and He knows they are for our greatest benefit. He has glorious rewards waiting for us in heaven, and He wants us to have every one of them. He

---

100 *You have been born again not of seed which is perishable but imperishable, that is, through the living and enduring word of God. For "all flesh is like grass, and all its glory like the flower of grass. The grass withers, and the flower falls off, but the word of the Lord endures forever." 1 Peter 1:23-25*

101 *"For I know the plans that I have for you," declares the LORD, "PLANS FOR WELFARE AND NOT FOR CALAMITY, TO GIVE YOU A FUTURE AND A HOPE."* Jeremiah 29:11

uses every situation, person, and thought to guide us toward obedience to His Word so we will gain them. Our time on earth is brief, no more substantial than a vapor He tells us.[102] But we'll be in heaven forever. We'd better forget empty earthly pleasures and concentrate on being prepared to stand before Christ at His Evaluation Throne and gain gold, silver and precious stones.[103]

Mike: We've said this several times, but it bears repeating: To die is gain. That whole concept of promotion to heaven excites me. If God says that when I die I have gained, how can I approach death with anything but a smile?

Tom: About that pivotal verse in Philippians 1:21, E.M. Bounds wrote, "Heaven ought to draw and engage us. Heaven ought to so fill our hearts and characters that all would see that we are strangers to this world, natives of a land fairer than this. We must be out of tune with this world. The very atmosphere of earth should be chilling to us, and its companionship dull and insipid. Heaven is our home, and death to us is birth. Heaven should kindle desire and, like a magnet, draw us upward to the sky. Duty, to God alone, should hold us here… Home—sacred, dear, restful, delightful, and full of holy feelings and deathless ties. In heaven, these will be ten thousand times stronger and sweeter."

Mike: I can't express myself nearly so well, but I know that I don't have anything other than God's will to hold me here on earth. I don't have to worry about my wife because He will take care of her. He'll take care of all those I love. My heart goes out to those who will weep. I want to assist them, but in the final analysis, God has already taken

---

102 *Yet you do not know what your life will be like tomorrow. You are just a vapor that appears for a little while and then vanishes away.* James 4:14

103 *For no man can lay a foundation other than the one which is laid, which is Jesus Christ. Now if any man builds on the foundation with gold, silver, precious stones, wood, hay, straw, each man's work will become evident for the day will show it because it is to be revealed with fire, and the fire itself will test the quality of each man's work.* 1Corinthians 3:11-13

care of it. Our job is to be available to Him until our last breath and to be excited that we're still in His plan and that His plan will promote us to heaven at the right time.

Tom: So why did we take time from our rapidly diminishing lives to write this book? If our book is given to someone who has just learned he has a terminal illness, we hope it will encourage him to face dying as just an inevitable part of life, an exciting part to be sure for a believer.

Mike: Not the end of him but a beginning full of perfection. If we live life knowing we will be promoted to heaven soon, looking it right square in the eye, we face a decision. Will we treat our suffering as a normal part of life, or will we exaggerate its importance?

Tom: This book puts on record that two believers have faced death with confidence, joy, peace, and contentment, and so can you.

The LORD is compassionate and gracious, slow to anger and abounding in lovingkindness [unfailing love]. *He will not always strive with us, nor will He keep His anger forever. He has not dealt with us according to our sins nor rewarded us according to our iniquities. For as high as the heavens are above the earth, so great is His lovingkindness toward those who fear Him. As far as the east is from the west, so far has He removed our transgressions from us. Just as a father has compassion on his children, so the LORD has compassion on those who fear Him, for He Himself knows our frame. He is mindful that we are but dust. As for man, his days are like grass. As a flower of the field, so he flourishes. When the wind has passed over it, it is no more, and its place acknowledges it no longer. But the lovingkindness of the LORD is from everlasting to everlasting on those who fear Him, and His righteousness to children's children, to those who keep His covenant and remember His precepts to do them. Psalm 103:13-18*

Dear Reader,

If you have just found out that you are dying, you need to assess your life to be sure you are going to heaven. Have you believed that Jesus Christ died on the cross as *your* substitute, taking your punishment for your sins, and that He was raised from the dead three days later and now sits at the right hand of God the Father in heaven? If you haven't, we have bad news for you. The pain you are experiencing now is nothing compared to the unending agony awaiting you in the Lake of Fire and Brimstone. Don't be a fool! Believe in Jesus Christ as your Savior right now, this very moment. After you die, you won't be able to change your mind even though you'll scream to do so. Believe now before it is too late!

If you know that Jesus Christ is your Savior and have been told you will face eternity in short order but aren't sure you are prepared for it, immerse yourself in God's Word so you can share in His peace and joy. Read, read, and reread your Bible. You'll be so glad you did. Your mind will be off your physical sufferings and on the One who has prepared a glorious place for you with Him. You'll rejoice in your weakness. You'll approach death with a smile on your face.

We want you, dear reader, to know with certainty that Jesus Christ will guide you through dying, that He will be just as faithful to you as He has been to us. We pray you will choose to grab hold of His promises for eternity and never let them go. Then, the greatest possible peace and joy will usher you into eternity with your living, loving God.

We will be waiting for you in heaven!

Your friends in Christ,

Mike McKinnon

Tom Northcott

To God be all glory!

EPILOGUE

God's Amazing Grace as Mike Is Promoted Home
by Patsy McKinnon

In November, 2005, God allowed Mike & me to begin the most incredible journey of our lifetime. We could never have imagined the spiritual growth we would experience and the blessings we would receive! From the very beginning to the very end of Mike's illness, God's power was always there for us to utilize, and His unfailing love surrounded us at all times. In fact, I could "write a book" just on this subject—but I will spare you!

Throughout this journey, Mike's hunger for God's Word continually increased. He maintained a joyful heart, peace, and contentment in God's perfect will as well as in God's perfect timing. Just two weeks before Mike was promoted to heaven, he sang the song "Until Then" [see page 38] at Albany Bible Church. The lyrics of the song were apropos in expressing Mike's joy and thoughts in the midst of his difficulties. During his last week, as soon as he was stabilized in the hospital, he motioned for me to get some Bible doctrine going! We listened to media, and the girls read to him from the book Catching a Glimpse of Heaven by E. M. Bounds that Tom had loaned him. Less than 24 hours before his promotion home, Mike was moved to Willson Hospice House in Albany.

On the evening of January 27, the Holy Spirit brought to my remembrance many things Mike had expressed to me in the previous two weeks, one of which was his desire that I would not have to see him struggle for his last breath. God the Holy Spirit kept working in me about Mike's desire, and I prayed fervently that I would make the right decision. When our pastor and his wife came to visit the morning of January 28, I talked to him about Mike's desire. I also discussed it with the hospice nurses and our nurse daughter, Cindy. They all assured me that more often than not a dying patient lets go after a loved one leaves the room. After intensely seeking God's guidance once again, I made the decision to leave for a couple of hours.

After informing the girls of my decision, I asked for a private moment with Mike. Although he could not talk to me, I fully believe he could hear every word I said. I told him I was going to leave for a couple of hours and go to our home (which he dearly loved) and just sit and reflect on the wonderful grace and mercies God had extended to us through all the years we had together. I encouraged him to let go and rest in God's perfect timing and assured him that I would be just fine.

With that, I left—with no reluctance, no fear, and no regret. I sat in our den, smiling and reflecting, praying and giving thanks to our gracious Father. Mike was taking his last breath as I pulled into the parking lot at Willson Hospice. Cindy & Lori were holding his hands while Jennifer read from Catching a Glimpse of Heaven. The words he heard from that book as he was promoted were the following: "We must destroy our infatuation with our earthly homes so that we seek a home in heaven." Then the author quoted a poem by William Hunter:

> "My heavenly home is bright and fair:
>
> No pain or death can enter there;
>
> Its glittering towers the sun outshine;
>
> That heavenly mansion shall be mine.

Let others seek a home below;

Which flames devour or waves o'erflow;

Be mine the happier lot to own

A heavenly mansion near the throne."

The girls waited five minutes after Mike passed to come get me. I was sitting in the car on the phone with Mike's brother, Greg, discussing arrangements for Mike's celebration of life. When Lori came out and told me the news, I burst into exclamations of happiness and thanksgiving for God's mercy and grace once again! How could Mike's promotion have been more awesome!

If that were not enough of God's comfort and peace and showering of blessings, I am compelled to tell you of one more incident on the day after Mike's promotion. While in the car driving to the funeral home, I decided to turn on the radio to a Christian station. Only on rare occasions have I turned on the car radio. Velda Goodman (the Goodman Family) was just beginning to sing a song entitled "Standing in the Presence of the King." I have included the words to that song below because I believe they were one way God provided even more comfort to me in the void I had now experienced in Mike's leaving his earthly home. Along with tears, I rejoiced that Mike was now truly standing in the presence of the King!!!!

Mike has now completed his journey and has reached his final destination in his eternal heavenly home. He is now experiencing the fulfillment of one of his favorite bible verses, Philippians 1:21: "For to me, to live is Christ and to die is gain."

Michael Johnathan McKinnon died happy!

Standing in the Presence of the King

Today I found myself in a most unusual place
All at once I was standing face to face
With someone that I knew so well yet I had never seen
I was standing in the presence of The King.

Standing in the presence of The King
The world just slips away beneath my feet;
Mortal man could never write the song that my heart sings
When I'm standing in the presence of The King.

Through His gates with thanksgiving into His courts with praise
With a joyous heart I begin to bless His name.
For at last I am standing where He said that I would be,
I am standing in the presence of The King.
Standing in the presence of The King
The world just slips away beneath my feet;
Mortal man could never write the song that my heart sings
When I'm standing in the presence of The King.

CPSIA information can be obtained at www.ICGtesting.com
Printed in the USA
LVOW10s0701170614

390272LV00002B/2/P